Wake up...
Live the Life You Love,

On The
Enlightened Path

Wake up... Live the Life You Love,

Little Seed Publishing, LLC
P.O. Box 4483
Laguna Beach, CA 92652

Pre-Press Management by TAE Marketing Consultations
Robert Valentine, Publications Director;
Lori Powell, Editorial Coordinator;
Rita Robinson, Accounts Manager.

Text Design: Wm. Gross Magee

Cover Illustrations: Klansee Bell

For information, contact Little Seed Publishing,
P.O. Box 4483, Laguna Beach, CA 92652,
or phone 562-884-0062

Distributed by Global Partnership, LLC
100 North 6th Street, Suite A
Murray, KY 42071

Library of Congress Cataloguing-In-Publication Data
ISBN: 1-933063-03-3

$14.95 USA $24.95 Canada

On The Enlightened Path

Other books by Steven E

Wake Up...Live the Life You Love

Wake Up...Live the Life You Love, Second Edition

Wake Up...Shape Up...Live the Life You Love

Wake Up...Live the Life You Love,
Inspirational How-to Stories

Wake Up...Live the Life You Love, In Beauty

Wake Up...Live the Life You Love,
Living on Purpose

Wake Up...Live the Life You Love,
Finding Your Life's Passion

Wake Up...Live the Life You Love,
Purpose, Passion, Abundance

Wake Up...Live the Life You Love,
Finding Personal Freedom

Wake Up...Live the Life You Love,
Seizing Your Success

Wake Up...Live the Life You Love,
Giving Gratitude

For your free gift, go to: **www.wakeupand.com**

Wake up... Live the Life You Love,

On The Enlightened Path

How would you like to be in the next book with a fabulous group of best-selling authors? Another Wake Up book is coming soon!

Visit: WakeUpLive.com

We would like to provide you with a free gift to enhance this book experience. For your free gift, please visit: WakeUpGift.com

Wake up... Live the Life You Love,

On The Enlightened Path

Dedication

*To those who walk The Enlightened Path
and show the way.*

Wake up... Live the Life You Love,

On The Enlightened Path

Contents

Forward xiii
    By Pamela Harper

Our Enlightened Path 1
    Pamela Harper

The First Agreement:Be Impeccable with Your Word 5
    don Miguel Ruiz

E=MC², One of "History's Mysteries" 7
    Sarah Chloe Burns

We Did It Together 11
    John and Michelle Humphrey

Finding Your Path 15
    Stephen A. Burgess

Doorway to Awakening 19
    Anita Bolen Collins

New Agreements for My New Life 23
    Sara Gilman

Embrace Silence 27
    Dr. Wayne Dyer

Your Success is a Decision Away! 29
    Stephen Gregg

Journey to the Self: Wisdom of Sufism
and Psychotherapy as a Path to Enlightenment 33
    Rahmana Lynn Larkin

For your free gift, go to: **www.wakeupand.com**

Wake up... Live the Life You Love,

Awaken the Inner Energy! 37
    Dr. Lana Marconi

Why Am I Here? 41
    Deepak Chopra

Sing Your Own Song 43
    Dede Morse

Life's Greatest Secret 47
    Dave O'Connor

Listen To Your Dreams 51
    Carolyn P. Reynolds

My Journey Toward Enlightenment...
from Modeling to Ministry 55
    Dr. Mina J. Sirovy

My Enlightened Path 59
    Colin Smith

The Voice of Beauty 63
    Deborah Striker

How I Found My Enlightened Path 65
    Jodi M. Valdes

The Enlightened ABC's 69
    Christian Wasinger

My Calling to be an Awakening Celebrant 73
    Bruce Winkle

A Blessing in Disguise 77
    Sharon Shohreh Javdan

You Can Harness Your Stress 81
    Christina Reynolds Goncalves

Our Perception Determines Our Experience 85
    Gregory Scott Reid

Through the Tunnel of Life 89
    Brandt Morgan

On The Enlightened Path

From Loser...to Leader...to Lover 93
  Charles Hai Nguyen

Guided by Divine Light 97
  Laurelle Shanti Gaia

Buttered Biscuits 101
  Yolande Nicholson-Spears

Path 105
  Nasrin Salehi

The Path of Possibilities 109
  Jacqueline Lynch

The First Essence of Life,
"Our Body the Foundation" 113
  Garry Choy

Wake up... Live the Life You Love,

Forward
By Pamela Harper

When Steven E and I first envisioned this special edition of the Wake Up Live series, we knew that we would attract dedicated and determined Souls ready to share their talents, tools, and words of wisdom, perfecting this momentous opportunity with the power of Unified Love.

The contributing authors in this book have gathered their passion, purpose, and prose so that all of God's creatures may prosper in loving peace, physical health, and financial wealth. We share these treasures of collective Truth to awaken, inspire, and illuminate *your* Enlightened Path.

Wake up... Live the Life You Love,

On The Enlightened Path

Our Enlightened Path
Pamela Harper

I began interviewing amazingly gifted people in my first career as a journalist. Traveling with politicians and celebrities inspired me to investigate their successful traits and tendencies. Continuing education and experience in the mind/body healing professions allowed collaboration with some of the world's most exceptional clinicians and healers. I noted that, in all cases, remarkable individuals lead exceptional lives; never deterred, always humble, and naturally abundant. The co-authors in this book series are among my favorite and most admired associates and friends for the blessed contributions and positive enhancements they present to our world.

To a greater degree, my affiliations have always been self-serving. I wanted to understand and then duplicate the apparent effortlessness at which the *masters* secure magic in every moment—to reap health, wealth, and unbounded joy. I am reminded each day by my Creator that I have agreed to devote my tireless energies to empowering, uniting, and promoting determined seekers of healing truth. I awake to the voice of directed wisdom, ready to move mountains so that architects of world peace and prosperity arrive on time, in divine order. We are all co-creators. We see ourselves in every other human being. We are the *chosen* ones, never resisting the relentless desire to rise above the mundane and ensure that the course of

Wake up... Live the Life You Love,

destiny is molded from *our* idea of the perfect world. We celebrate your decision to exceed your greatest expectations and join us on *our Enlightened Path.*

There Are No Sanctioned Exits on the Enlightened Path

How do you know when you are traveling the Enlightened Path? There are designated signposts along the way. Once afoot, you remain alert and steadfast. A wrong turn here or there is like a jump off a ledge of the Grand Canyon. Whoa! You don't ever want to get that close to the edge. Your heart pounds and thoughts are racing.

Your perfect body is designed to sound the alarm when you are veering off the path. Stop! Look out; those old limiting thoughts are mounting in an attempt to repeat the past and remain in the favored certainty of the status quo even if it means physical death or mental anguish. You daringly decide to risk it all as you deflect the noticeable discomfort, sidestep *disease*, and regain optimal health. Fear thoughts are immediately replaced by blind faith.

There is a moment in time when the Path is all there is and there is no turning back. Posterior eyesight does not exist. The uplifting force of the Enlightened Path blocks the view of any exit signs. You are One with your Sacred Journey, destined to use your talents and gifts to perpetuate Goodness and unlimited possibilities.

Enlightened Beings Do <u>Not</u> Have Problems

If you invite enlightened beings to share in the energy of chaos or frenzy of dilemmas and discontent they will decline and comment, "I never noticed there was a problem. I was awaiting solutions." They establish a proactive mindset. They know that one cannot engage in two

On The Enlightened Path

opposing thoughts at a time, so they will always opt for the vision that promotes perpetual bliss.

Happy people perpetuate pleasure. It's not that they are indifferent to poor, suffering souls; it's just more beneficial to focus on acceptance and solutions. Contrary to the guilt-laden ego, we cannot alleviate the pain or suffering of another by sacrificing our own peace of mind. People who attend to higher consciousness will gladly offer a smile and a model of being, but will never forgo their own sense of well-being. Health, wealth, and eternal paradise are never furthered by expanding the population of the pitifully perplexed.

Prosperity Flows

Enlightened beings believe that if they do what they love, not only does money grow on trees but it blooms in every moment spent in pursuit of greatness. They are also ready, willing, and able to assist others in building bridges to their personal prosperous path.

The source of all goodness is never in question, nor is the probability of prosperity. If you ask them if they are worried about the state of the economy, they will tell you that they most certainly foresee plenty. Many of my enlightened associates have admittedly escaped from states of poor thinking and modest money. Because we knew that to complete our projects we required ample cash, we gladly released the daily struggle inherent in a life of poverty.

The Path Is Paved with Purpose

Purposeful people share ideas and talents to make a difference for now and all time. They never question how or when it will happen. In the course of talking to the

Wake up... Live the Life You Love,

co-authors of this book, I was consistently impressed by their tenacity, determination, and single-mindedness of purpose. Unlimited vision secures the future. When you know where you're going, the destination and outcome are always in view.

Miracles Commonly Occur

Daily decisions are determined by great expectations and divine guidance. The higher self is navigating purposeful and productive goals. Pure thought separates intuition from indecision. The only difference between great leaders and everyone else is that they believe the voice in the wind. The Enlightened Path sustains momentum and eliminates doubt.

Awakened doers never wonder whether their prayers are answered. They know that the purpose of meditation and prayer is to communicate with the Creator in the here and now. They make conscious contact with Creation and expect their order to be filled upon request. These are the moments of our making in God-centered thinking.

Please Join in Future Events

Our collective efforts are not limited to this book. We are planning events and projects that capitalize on our commitment to healing the world with thought and deed.

Please join us.

ꙮPamela Harper, RN, CCH, CAC

On The Enlightened Path

The First Agreement:
Be Impeccable with Your Word
don Miguel Ruiz

The first agreement is the most important one and also the most difficult one to honor. It is so important that with just this first agreement you will be able to transcend to the level of existence I call heaven on earth.

The first agreement is to *be impeccable with your word.* It sounds very simple, but it is very, very powerful.

Why your word? Your word is the power that you have to create. Your word is the gift that comes directly from God. The Gospel of John in the Bible, speaking of the creating of the universe, says, "In the beginning was the word, and the word was with God, and the word is God." Through the word you express your creative power. It is through the word that you manifest everything. Regardless of what language you speak, your intent manifests through the word. What you dream, what you feel, and what you really are, will all be manifested through the word.

The word is not just a sound or a written symbol. The word is a force; it is the power you have to express and communicate, to think, and thereby to create the events in your life. You can speak. What other animal on the planet can speak? The word is the most powerful tool you have as a human; it is the tool of magic. But like a sword

Wake up... Live the Life You Love,

with two edges, your word can create the most beautiful dream, or your word can destroy everything around you. One edge is the misuse of the word, which creates a living hell. The other edge is the impeccability of the word, which will only create beauty, love, and heaven on earth. Depending upon how it is used, the word can set you free, or it can enslave you even more than you know. All the magic you possess is based on your word. Your word is pure magic, and misuse of your word is black magic.

The word is so powerful that one word can change a life or destroy the lives of millions of people. Some years ago one man in Germany, by the use of the word, manipulated a whole country of the most intelligent people. He led them into a world war with just the power of his word. He convinced others to commit the most atrocious acts of violence. He activated people's fear with the word, and like a big explosion, there was killing and war all around the world. All over the world humans destroyed other humans because they were afraid of each other. Hitler's word, based on fear-generated beliefs and agreements, will be remembered for centuries.

The human mind is like a fertile ground where seeds are continually being planted. The seeds are opinions, ideas and concepts. You plant a seed, a thought, and it grows. The word is like a seed, and the human mind is so fertile! The only problem is that too often it is fertile for the seeds of fear. Every human mind is fertile, but only for those kinds of seeds it is prepared for. What is important is to see which kind of seeds our mind is fertile for, and to prepare it to receive the seeds of love.

cx/cy don Miguel Ruiz

On The Enlightened Path

E=MC², One of "History's Mysteries"
Sarah Chloe Burns

*R*ight now, you may be asking yourself what a quantum physics equation formulated by a German scientist a century ago (1905) has to do with the idea of today's enlightened spirituality. For those of you who tend to slip into a coma at the very mention of the word "history," the temptation to skip over this article may be painfully strong. However, I urge each of you to read on, entertaining the prospect that the distant past indeed lives side-by-side with today's world. In fact, the "relative" possibility for each of us to test this time/space theory on a daily basis will soon become abundantly clear. Please, allow me to enlighten you.

Albert Einstein rocked the world of the early 20th century by positing his theories of "Special" and "General" Relativity. In essence, he proposed that the passage of time and measurement of distance is not absolute. His proof is as follows. As a clock approaches a mass (i.e., the sun), it begins to tick more slowly, due to the changing effects of gravity. Likewise, gravitational pull not only bends starlight but also acts as a powerful suction cup. The sudden collapse of mass results in such an immense oppositional force that anything sucked inside can never escape (Black Hole Theory). So what do these ever-expanding and elastic quantum physics theories have to

Wake up... Live the Life You Love,

do with historical facts? In my own experience, every-thing! If time and space are so relative, our own inten-tions and projections—projections powerful enough—can position us in circumstances of which we might otherwise only dream. Read on, my friend.

In July 2002, while conducting research throughout England and Scotland for my first historical novel, one of my most important trips was to the prominent town of Oxford, England. Within the context of my story line, I had created a fictional character who was attending Pembroke College in 1638 (today, it is one of Oxford's 39 colleges). My purpose in Oxford that summer was to walk the hallowed grounds upon which I had placed young James Campbell. In one dramatic day in 1638, amidst emotional turmoil, he reminisced at his dorm window, staring across the commons. His thoughts so frightened him that he raced down the stairs, across the grounds of Christ Church and Magdalen Colleges, toward Holiwell Church—where he prayed fervently for hours.

After touring Oxford by bus and locating the College, I was anxious to enter Pembroke and trace James's path. Unfortunately for me, the public was not admitted to any of the college commons areas on that day; furthermore, it would be extremely rare and fortunate for anyone other than students or their parents or tutors to do so on any other day of the year. Only very special circumstances would pave the way for such an excursion. As I sadly climbed some nearby steps and hung from the wall sur-rounding Pembroke, I peered from a distance, attempting to absorb the ancient atmosphere, while snapping photos. I had driven for hours, handled a stick shift from the

On The Enlightened Path

right side of a van, driving on the left side of the road—placing hundreds of drivers in peril—just to catch this mere glimpse. Mentally, I placed myself within Pembroke.

In November 2002, while still teaching at Bakersfield College, as well as lecturing at California State University, Bakersfield, I received an invitation to participate in the Oxford Roundtable on Human Rights and Gender Discrimination (to be held March 30 – April 4, 2003). Delighted at the prospect, I prepared an abstract and submitted it in a timely manner. Fortunately, my topic was chosen. Not only would I attend—I would be a presenter. How grand!

As I made preparations to return to Oxford (only eight months after my first visit), I received notification from the Oxford Roundtable group that the invitees attending this session had grown to such a great number that we would have to be divided among three college campuses. Instead of being quartered within Exeter College, my particular group would be housed and hosted by—you guessed it—Pembroke College. I could hardly believe my good fortune! Furthermore, upon arrival at Oxford and Pembroke on March 30, I was handed another great gift. Because I had registered early for this "Think Tank," I was given one of the best locations—a dorm room on the third level, with two built-in window desks. The double windows above each desk opened widely onto the quad upon which I had gazed only the previous summer.

I believe Jesus said it best, "Ask, and it shall be given you; seek, and ye shall find; knock, and it shall be opened unto you." In July 2002, I stood at the door of all possibility, gazing upon an enduring earthly space and

Wake up... Live the Life You Love,

centuries-old institution. I focused my attention and intention upon the object of my desire. The universe in turn began immediately to cooperate and reorganize, in order to bring about the outcome I so desired. As a result, in less than a year, I was privileged to spend almost an entire week of my life within the very dorm room I had described in Chapter 11 of my book. Who says the age of miracles lies in the past? Albert Einstein and I know better—it's all relative!

❧Sarah Chloe Burns

On The Enlightened Path

We Did It Together
John and Michelle Humphrey

*A*s we pulled up to our new home, driving in our new car, we sat in wonder. Life could not be better. Our eyes filled with joyful tears as we took a moment to recall a vision of the journey that brought us to this moment. Our path to enlightenment and personal growth has finally paid off. But, for many years, while our determination to have a great life and grow together may have been strong, the results in our lives were so very disappointing.

Just seven years ago, if you had known us intimately, you would have probably bet all your money that we would not have made it as a couple. We were each "licking the wounds" of our hearts from failed marriages and struggling with money and our careers; the direction of our lives was uncertain. We were dating and living in separate apartments in New Jersey. The one thing we did have was a love for each other that was strong and real, but we wondered what would happen to our relationship in the coming months. Michelle wanted to move to San Diego for a better life and I was a native New Yorker, nestled in my roots.

Michelle, determined for a better life and more connection to like-minded people, turned to personal development. She attended and even crewed a wide variety of seminars. Feeling panicked and threatened by it all, I

Wake up... Live the Life You Love,

belittled Michelle's dreams and even tried to talk her out of going. Still Michelle was focused, and she knew she was not going to settle for less. Then, one day, I called her and told her that it had "hit" me like a ton of bricks. I understood why Michelle was determined to have a great life, and that I was completely onboard.

Our lives were typical: corporate jobs and not enough money. In the next couple of years, we became more "spiritual" and even went into business with a spiritual guru, entering the world of teaching personal development and seminars. Things seemed to be getting better and better, until a failed business venture left us $850,000 in debt. How could this happen? For months all we felt was scared and confused. The stress of it started affecting our relationship as well as our health. We had spent years focusing on making our lives better and now they were worse than ever. What happened? We thought we knew all about manifesting. Boy, were we wrong! We knew only the beginning. But what happened in the following months would change it all.

Michelle, even in the midst of all our problems, found out about a special training that dealt with learning to master control over your mind, how to quiet that mind chatter, and, most of all, how to "really" get in touch with the power that all the books and tapes were talking about, but which had eluded us time and time again. This seminar cost $25,000. Wow! It was hard to believe. Yet even with all the debt and few resources, Michelle was determined to go. She convinced her bank to loan her the money.

On The Enlightened Path

She went to the seminar and when she came back, the magic started to really happen. The $850,000 debt was gone in four months. We started multiple successful businesses and within one year, we started building our dream house. All the while, we drew closer and closer to each other. We now confidently share that the key to a great life comes from mastering your mind, and this key unlocked all the doors that were once closed. Michelle's results spoke for themselves; when I soon saw the power of the seminar, I also attended.

Together, we now teach people all over the world how to create a great life by using more of the mind. Best of all, it works. It is the only success system proven by independent university research.

Why do we tell you all this? Because there are many people caught in relationships where one person may want to engage in personal development, reaching for more in life, and the other is satisfied with his current life. We have found that this situation can make you better and can create an opening for both of you. We are together and thriving now because I allowed Michelle to follow her heart and she allowed me to come around in my own time. We now know, if couples will trust and allow their partners to go on their own divine paths, instead of judging each other and making each other wrong, they can enjoy a thriving relationship.

If you asked us seven years ago, "Do you think you two will be together, living your dream life, and helping others to do the same?" We would have said, "No way!" But that Life inside you will take you places you never thought possible.

Wake up... Live the Life You Love,

All we can say is, "Jump out! Play a bigger game, and grab that life you have been waiting to live." Be that inspirational story for others and change the world. It will be the best time of your life.

～John and Michelle Humphrey

On The Enlightened Path

Finding Your Path
Stephen A. Burgess

*O*nce in awhile you meet someone who knows what they want to do in life and who takes all the right steps to reach their ambitions and goals. I have great respect for those few who have this vision and can act on it and live such a fulfilling life. Not only do they seem to be few and far between, but all data show they are a true rarity.

Those who have found their path and followed it are easy to spot but hard to find. They are easy to spot because it seems so obvious to everyone who meets them that they are living a life of purpose and fulfillment. They are hard to find because they are so rare.

For most of my life I was one of the many and not one of the few. Why? I think because I didn't know what my path was, or because I put up obstacles to keep from finding my path.

For me, it was first the "not knowing" stage. I came out of college and didn't really know what I wanted to do or be. I started down a path and hoped it would lead somewhere. And it did!

I went into business and because of my work ethic, personal drive to succeed, and some wise (and even lucky) choices, I became a successful executive, leading fast-growing companies and turning others around. I also had a growing family. Yet, despite a series of accomplishments that many would envy, I didn't feel really fulfilled. I

Wake up... Live the Life You Love,

always felt I was on the wrong path—I was missing *something*, but I did not know what.

After 20 years of senior executive experience and success, I was in the process of exiting my last group of companies and began the process of looking for my next opportunity. I believed this opportunity would look like the others: turning around or leading a high-growth company.

In my search for a position I found myself very close to accepting a new assignment. In fact, I was told I would be flying out to receive my offer, Chief Operating Officer of a multi-national company. I would be responsible for North America, Asia, and Australia.

Despite being the only candidate left for the position (all others had been eliminated), I was very surprised to find that the company had decided to go in a different direction and the position was no longer available. My most trusted friend and advisor, my wife, told me that she felt it was meant to be. I was not supposed to take this position; I was meant to do something else. Somehow I knew she was right. It was as if the flood gates opened. Suddenly, I had all these ideas of things I wanted to do but had put aside because I didn't have time, had a family to raise, had a career to build, and all the other justifications I had learned so well.

For the first time, I *ignored* all of them!

I could see a path but could not fully visualize it. Then, as if it was meant to be, I met someone who was a visualization expert.

Pamela Harper and I sat down one afternoon and in just 30 minutes she helped me create and see my vision—my path! I was to be a best-selling author, a noted speaker,

On The Enlightened Path

a coach, and have my own consulting business helping others succeed. And I could *SEE* it!

Just months later I was co-author of a #1 best-selling book, had spoken at more than a dozen engagements, and was coaching and consulting others to help them succeed through my knowledge and experience. I had found my *enlightened path!*

How can you find yours? Go with your "gut" feeling, don't be afraid to follow what seems right, because it usually is.

Find a trusted advisor and listen. My wife has been a source of truth and vision, and I have learned to listen to the person who knows me best. Find a mentor, coach, or person who can help you visualize your path. I found Pamela Harper to be of particular assistance to me. Her ability to help me see my path was extraordinary and invaluable.

Finally, don't let your fears and "old" beliefs keep you from your path. Block out those that would stop you with their negative influence. You can do it, and the view from the other side is *beautiful!*

℘Stephen A. Burgess

Wake up... Live the Life You Love,

On The Enlightened Path

Doorway to Awakening
Anita Bolen Collins

*I*t's very clear in my memory that I "woke up" on November 12, 2003, at 1:20 in the afternoon. By learning to use one simple tool that day, I opened the door to a joyful new way of living.

The Call

I had planned to participate in the Effortless Living Institute's question-and-answer teleconference on November 12 at 1:00 p.m. On that afternoon I went out for lunch. When I returned at 1:20, I realized that the teleconference had already started. Should I forget about calling in since I was late for the session? Something urged me to call anyway.

Quickly, I dialed the phone number. My call connected immediately and I heard the voice of Michelle Humphrey, a Master Mentor, describing a muscle testing technique to determine truth from falsehood. I listened with interest. *Is it possible that anyone, at any time, can know the truth in any situation?*

I knew that health practitioners, such as kinesiologists, use muscle testing to determine unbalances in the body, especially food allergies. You may have seen this two-person technique: the client's arm is outstretched parallel to the ground and the practitioner applies pressure on the arm to measure resistance. I thought to myself, "Yes, muscle testing works but how can you get results when you

Wake up... Live the Life You Love,

are by yourself? Besides, wouldn't this relate only to health issues?" The answers to these questions surprised me.

Michelle quoted research from the book *Power vs. Force* by David R. Hawkins, which states that "the individual mind is like a computer terminal connected to a giant database and the database is human consciousness itself." Muscle testing within your own body becomes the gateway through which your higher self can access absolute truth from the infinite field of consciousness. We are all connected and all knowledge is available to us.

A New Tool

The body doesn't lie. The muscle testing tool that I learned can be used anywhere, at anytime, and by oneself. It's a reliable technique that allows your body to reveal the answer to a clearly stated "yes" or "no" question simply by trusting and feeling.

With this new tool I had access to an easy, personal, accurate, and portable system to know the truth and eliminate uncertainty! I practiced the technique as soon as the call ended and was elated with the results.

To begin, I stood up, cleared my mind, and stated my name. I said aloud, "My name is Anita." What did I feel happening in my body? Like a tree gently swaying in the wind, my whole body started to lean forward because it's true, my name is Anita. What about when I substitute someone else's name? I said aloud, "My name is John." Just as Michelle said would happen, my whole body tipped or leaned backward since this is not true about me.

The Possibilities

How could I use this tool? Laughing with delight, I realized the options were infinite. I could ask the universe any yes/no question and my higher self would reveal the

On The Enlightened Path

answer for my greatest good. Making decisions would forever be effortless. Now I am able to get organized easily at home or at the office: which actions are for the highest good of myself and others today? In my commute: which highway route avoids traffic jams? What to wear in the morning: my higher self selects the best outfit. At meal time: which foods best nourish my body today? Decorating: what color of paint or drapes best suit this room? The answers I receive are always perfect.

Everything matters and everything is connected. I welcome and allow my higher self to guide me on every decision, issue, and action. Often, what might be considered a routine or mundane question leads me to a better and more enjoyable outcome than I would have chosen on my own. The question, "What time should I go to the library?" led me to go much later than I had planned one day. I just happened to walk through the door at the same time as an old friend I hadn't seen in nearly ten years. Divine order and timing continually unfold.

Awakening

I became aware that I can make choices each and every moment. Where do I direct my attention right now for the highest good of all? My confidence, trust, and intuition expand daily. By listening to the body and bypassing the mind, ego, and past opinions or judgments, a beautiful dance takes place between the universe and my higher self. I feel that each day is a gift co-created with God.

Everyone can connect with their higher self to live a life filled with joy, peace, love, and prosperity. Muscle testing and listening to your own body is an easy way to start.

ᏘᎦAnita Bolen Collins

Wake up... Live the Life You Love,

On The Enlightened Path

New Agreements for My New Life
Sara Gilman

*H*ave you ever found yourself walking through your life wondering, "Why are things not going the way I'd like? I'm working hard. I'm writing my goals, taking action, going to seminars to expand my learning." People described me as having a lot of energy, yet I was constantly fighting a sense of underlying fatigue and the troubling question, "Can I keep this up?" Instead of having more time for myself, my life seemed to be getting busier as I got older, resulting in more effort just to maintain the status quo.

As a single mother of two teenage boys and a psychotherapist in private practice, I "worked" at maintaining a healthy balance in my life. I wasn't always successful. Then one day I heard a speaker who spoke directly to my weary heart. He said, "To change your world you must first change your mind. That's because your mind creates your reality or your 'world'". Wow! You mean all I have to do is change my mind and my life will be more successful, fulfilling, and easier? I know how to do that; I have changed my mind many times! I bought David Dibble's wonderful book*, The New Agreements in the Workplace – Releasing the Human Spirit.*

I soon found that what David was really talking about was "transforming my mind" into a wonderful vehicle of love, clarity, and focus. As a coach myself, I knew

Wake up... Live the Life You Love,

that to truly transform, I needed a coach, a true teacher who could guide me. I began working with this amazing teacher.

The basis of this work began with understanding the five New Agreements: (1) Find your path; (2) Love, grow, and serve your people; (3) Mind your mind in the moment; (4) Shift your systems; (5) Practice a little every day. We dove into these areas through a unique type of dream work, focusing on the four parts of the mind (masculine, feminine, authoritarian, and spiritual), and through understanding character types, which describe how individuals think and process information.

After 25 years as a therapist and coach, I had never experienced such deep transformative work that so easily translated into life changes. My mind became clearer and I made decisions more easily. Taking action in the most important areas of my life is no longer draining; it is fun, energizing, and fulfilling. New, exciting ideas pop into my consciousness regularly. I am using sleep time as time for transformation as I dream! My inner energy and outer moods are brighter and more consistent. I am attracting what I really want and I am accomplishing more than I could have ever imagined. Learning to connect deeply and consistently with my own inner wisdom (inner spirit) has provided me with validation and newfound energy! It's as if a wellspring of peaceful energy continues to fill me and flow from me.

I want you to experience what I am experiencing! You are reading these pages because you too, want your life and heart to grow with feelings of fulfillment and joy. I want that for you, too! These are the most valuable steps I have taken to create my new life:

On The Enlightened Path

1. Find the teacher, coach, counselor, or guide who is your teacher.

2. Take time every day to sit quietly in meditation. Just sit, focusing on your breathing and quieting your mind. Over time you will be surprised how this helps you grow.

3. Discover what your path and purpose are in this life-time; Live it fully.

4. Explore what The New Agreements might mean for you and how you might easily apply them to your life, both at work and at home.

5. Keep a journal where you write your thoughts and dreams and the new insights that will surely come to you.

6. Take action every day—practice a little every day. Live, Love, Laugh!

ev Sara Gilman

Wake up... Live the Life You Love,

On The Enlightened Path

Embrace Silence
Dr. Wayne Dyer

You live in a noisy world, constantly bombarded with loud music, sirens, construction equipment, jet airplanes, rumbling trucks, leaf blowers, lawn mowers, and tree cutters. These manmade, unnatural sounds invade your sense and keep silence at bay.

In fact, you've been raised in a culture that not only eschews silence, but is terrified of it. The car radio must always be on, and any pause in conversation is a moment of embarrassment that most people quickly fill with chatter. For many, being alone in silence is pure torture.

The famous scientist Blaise Pascal observed, "All man's miseries derive from not being able to sit quietly in a room alone."

The Value of Silence

With practice, you can become aware that there's a momentary silence in the space between your thoughts. In this silent space, you'll find the peace that you crave in your daily life. You'll never know that peace if you have no spaces between your thoughts.

The average person is said to have 60,000 separate thoughts every day. With so many thoughts, there are almost no gaps. If you could reduce that number by half, you would open up an entire world of possibilities for yourself. For it is when you merge in the silence and become one with it that you reconnect to your source and

Wake up... Live the Life You Love,

know the peacefulness that some call God. "Be still and know that I am God," says it so beautifully in Psalms of the Old Testament. The key words are "still" and "know."

"Still" actually means silence. Mother Theresa described silence and its relationship to God by saying, "God is the friend of Silence. See how nature—trees, grass—grow in silence; see the stars, the moon and the sun—how they move in silence. We need silence to be able to touch souls." This includes your soul!

It's really the space between the notes that makes the music you enjoy so much. Without the spaces, all you would have is one continuous noisy note. Everything that's created comes out of silence. Your thoughts emerge from the nothingness of silence. Your words come out of this void. Your very essence emerged from emptiness.

Those who will supersede us are waiting in the vast void. All creativity requires some stillness. Your sense of inner peace depends on spending some of your life energy in silence to recharge your batteries, and remove tension and anxiety, thus reacquainting you with the joy of knowing God and feeling closer to all of humanity. Silence reduces fatigue and allows you to experience your own creative juices.

The second word in the Old Testament observation, "know," refers to making your personal and conscious contact with God. To know God is to banish doubt and become independent of others' definitions and descriptions of God. Instead, you have your own personal knowing. And, as Melville reminded us so poignantly, "God's one and only voice is silence."

ᘓ Dr. Wayne Dyer

On The Enlightened Path

Your Success is a Decision Away!
Stephen Gregg

*I*t was 1981, my freshmen year in high school. I remember watching my mother enter the Publishers' Clearing House Sweepstakes and telling me that, one day, we were going to win. Of course, it never happened. I also remember when the large, well- known electronics company made the decision that they didn't need my mother to work there anymore because college students would work for less money. I saw many struggles as a child, but those two events changed my life. *I made a decision* that I would never work a salaried job and that if I were to get rich it would be by hard work, not luck.

My journey began as a fashion designer. In high school I designed clothes and dreamed of creating my own line of clothing. I told my mother that one day I was going to make her rich and she would never have to work again. A few years later we moved to Los Angeles, California, where I attended the Fashion Design Institute of Design and Merchandising. I went for one year and then life took another turn; we ran out of money and I had to quit school. I got a job selling cars and, after three years, I went to work for Circuit City. One day a friend and I saw a video tape that changed my life's path forever.

The video was called "*Countering the Conspiracy to Destroy Black Boys.*" This video caused something inside

Wake up... Live the Life You Love,

me that I can't explain. Soon after, I saw a place off the freeway by downtown Los Angeles called Tent City. It was a place where the homeless could live in white tents for a period of time. After seeing these two things, *I made a decision* that *I* was going to make a difference in the world.

I created a program called Inner-Prize. It was to comprise a chain of community centers in every major city that would house workshops and seminars to help people in many different ways. Some of the topics were health education, family relationships, career development, job placement, abuse counseling, and recreational activities. I had the program written in such great detail that I knew it was going to happen and that it was just a matter of time. From then on, every job or business opportunity I pursued had to be leading to Inner-Prize. I went through 35 different jobs and businesses trying to earn the money to make this **hope** of mine become a reality. I failed miserably many times and I felt frustrated. I started to doubt that I could achieve my dream.

After years of frustration and many failed attempts, I finally got the blessing that I needed. I was given the opportunity to create my dream as a gift from God. Inner-Prize was born in July 2003, **12 years after it was originally created in my mind.** Inner-Prize is now being formulated and we believe that it will be a nationwide icon, the most benevolent nonprofit organization in the nation. We know that thousands of lives will be positively impacted by Inner-Prize.

It's amazing what can happen if you **set a big dream, believe** that it will come true, **remain faithful to God,** and **persevere** until you've achieved it. I hope you will

On The Enlightened Path

take the following three things from my story that can help you in your life.

- **Believe that you can create your path in life.** You should have a dream so big that it would take 10 lifetimes to achieve. God wouldn't give you a dream that you couldn't have.

- **Believe that you can make a difference.** I always believed that one person can make a difference, but after going through all of the challenges that I went through, I realized that my limiting belief was holding me back. Even though I did believe that one person could make a difference, I didn't believe that I could be that person. Then two people believed in me enough to allow me to grow and develop my talents, Steve Speichinger and Gary Ware of AFLAC. Because of their belief in me, I realized that I could make a difference. If you need a person like that in your life, call me and I'll be that person for you.

- **Make a decision** to change your life and begin to take action! You can do it. Believe me, if I could do it, so can you. **Your success is a decision away!**

ᑫᔆStephen Gregg

Wake up... Live the Life You Love,

Journey to the Self: Wisdom of Sufism and Psychotherapy as a Path to Enlightenment
Rahmana Lynn Larkin

"You think you are a small body, yet within you lies the greater Universe." —Amir al Momenin Ali

*M*y journey to myself has been primarily through psychotherapy and Sufism. As Amir al Momenin Ali suggests, I have discovered that the true self is not the limited personality or the small body with which people normally identify. Our essence is beyond anything we can imagine. We are already connected to the Divine and have unlimited potential of which we are unaware. This journey to the self *is* the path to enlightenment.

For me, the search for my true self began as a child. My family moved nine times before I left for college at age 17. With each move I stepped into a new environment in which others did not have preconceived notions of who I was. I found myself redefining the image I wanted to present to the world before my first day at each new school. By exploring these images of myself I began to notice my false self. Underneath this fluctuating sense of self-identity, I also saw glimpses of a deeper part of me (my essence) that was unchanging. My search for this unchanging place of peace led me to the world of psychology and to an exploration of a variety of spiritual perspectives. As a psychotherapist I often witness individuals

Wake up... Live the Life You Love,

opening up spiritually as they begin to consciously accept and love their false selves. As they recognize and work through ego issues they often become aware of a deeper part of themselves. This was true in my own therapy work, and Sufism was the next step in helping me to connect with, and live from this essence.

Sufism, the mystical branch of Islam, is a spiritual path composed of practical steps to knowing the Divine. Although Sufism is not well known in the West, many are familiar with the Sufi poet Rumi, whose wonderful poems of love draw from the wisdom of Sufism and the *Holy Qur'an*. The concept that God is everywhere and everything is the foundation of Sufism and Islam. Recognizing that everyone (including myself) is a reflection of the Divine has allowed me to be more loving both to others and to myself. Since God is everywhere, it is only our false self that causes us to feel separate. This separation blocks us from knowing our true essence and experiencing the love that is always around us.

Through meditation, prayer, and other practices, Sufism has provided me with concrete steps and guidance that have helped me to clear away this separation. These practices have helped me be more aware and able to move out of my mind and connect to my heart. In this place of awareness I am able to let go of judgments and experience peace and love even during difficult times. Over the years I have voraciously read one spiritual book after another, only to discover that spirituality cannot be learned through books or lectures. Our minds are incapable of knowing spiritual truths.

Sufism has given me the experience of being connected to amazing teachers (Shah Nazar Seyed Ali Kianfar and

On The Enlightened Path

Seyedeh Nahid Angha). Through their contact with the Divine they are able to provide accurate guidance as well as spiritual and emotional support. Through them I have learned about unconditional love and that I am much more than this small body. For years I have realized that the Divine can be found only within. Through Sufism I have learned the specific steps with which to make that discovery. This path has helped me to connect with my own inner guidance and my own spirituality. My teacher Dr. Kianfar, often reminds me that we are all on our own paths. It is up to each of us to discover that path. A true teacher will lead you to *your path* and not to his or hers.

We are all on a path to enlightenment. Enlightenment is found through discovering the true Self rather than by focusing on something outside of us. As the Sufi mystic Rumi said, "*You suppose that you're in trouble, but you're really the cure. You suppose that you're the lock on the door, but you're really the key that opens it. It's too bad that you want to be someone else. You don't see your own face, your own beauty. Yet, no one's face is more beautiful than yours.*" (Translation by Nevit Ergin)

Traveling this path of Self-discovery can be long and difficult. It is up to each of us to choose how far down this path we want to travel. Although I am far from my goal, I have traveled far enough to know that for me it is worth the journey.

ल৵Rahmana Lynn Larkin

Wake up... Live the Life You Love,

On The Enlightened Path

Awaken the Inner Energy!
Dr. Lana Marconi

Seven years ago on one May morning when I was twenty-three, I sat alone on my bedroom floor with my eyes closed. I shared with God (my perception of God at that time was from Christianity as opposed to spirituality) how sorry I was for forgetting "Him." I also shared with Him that I loved Him.

As my heart kept expressing its love to God, I was overcome with a powerful feeling of love inside me, and there was an incredible golden light that filled the interior space of my mind. Each time my heart expressed my love for Him, I would feel more love inside me. I also felt incredible peace.

Next, every cell of my entire being began expanding, being pulled further and further out from me in all directions. I was expanding into Infinite Love Light and dissolving into it. As more and more of me dissolved into the golden light, the "I" in me left!

When my awareness returned, I felt volumes of soothing and gentle energy pour into my body from above my head. It was as if I was sitting under a waterfall being showered with a soft flow of liquid Love and Light. The caressing energy poured into me for some time, maintaining the great love and peace I was feeling.

I then told God in my mind that I wanted to hug Him. The message I received back was to wrap my arms

Wake up... Live the Life You Love,

around myself. In silence I sat alone on the floor and held myself as energy continued to flow into me from Heaven, as love continued to overflow my heart, and as peace continued to take over my mind.

What had happened to me? I understood much later that I had awakened the evolutionary, divine energy known in Hinduism as *kundalini*. Once a person has kundalini surface, that energy brings to light the potentials resting dormant in his soul (commonly expanded using the Chakra System), including any and all archetypes such as the healer archetype and the homosexual archetype.

Six years passed during which I learned to manage and understand the inner fire goddess, kundalini, and embrace the karmic shadow material as it arose from the depths of my chakras. During this time, I completed a Ph.D. in Energy Medicine. In my seventh year, I synchronistically met a real guru, Yogi Ramesh, who introduced me to a woman shaman, Kahuna Sandra Rose Michael. Taking me under her wing, Dr. Michael nurtured me to further *live the life I awakened to love*: To assist with the Global Ascension in Consciousness. She developed the Energy Enhancement System™, (EES). Computers generate multiple bioactive life-enhancing energy fields, including "scalar waves," which can allow cell regeneration and increased immune function, provide relief from pain, detoxify the body, balance right and left brain hemispheres, increase energy levels, produce intimate meditative states, and other miraculous results.

As kundalini is referred to as the best inner psychotherapist, the EES is, in my experience, the best outer psychotherapist! People exposed to this powerful healing field

can expect *all* the emotional and mental *baggage* inside of them to surface for integration purposes within the psyche. As a field technology, every system that gets set up expands the field, facilitating the global rise in consciousness and wholeness. The EES was clairvoyant Sandra's spirit-guided answer to her question, "How do we create the quantum leap in consciousness where we can bypass projected future realities that didn't look pleasant, such as those that might have been worse than Nazi Germany?"

If you are not clear on how to consciously *live and love your purpose,* I recommend awakening kundalini to cleanse and purify your body, mind, and soul, and/or get yourself in an EES chamber right away to awaken your powerful inner energy!

℘Dr. Lana Marconi

Wake up... Live the Life You Love,

On The Enlightened Path

Why Am I Here?
Deepak Chopra

From an Interview with Dr. R. Winn Henderson

The majority of people on earth are unfulfilled or unhappy because they do not have a purpose or a mission. As a part of the human species, we seek purpose and meaning; we laugh, and we are aware of our mortality (that one day we will die). This is what distinguishes us from other creatures. Laughter, mortality, and purpose, become three important, crucial questions. We search for meaning—a deep significance to life.

Why am I here? Why have I been placed on the earth? We've been placed on earth to make a difference in life itself and in others' lives. In order to make a difference, we must find what we are good at and like to do and what benefits others.

We all have a mission, and my mission in life is to understand and explore consciousness and its various expressions, and also to share that with anyone who's interested in doing the same. It boils down to understanding the mechanics of healing, the rule of love. I would say, to put it very simply, my mission is to love, to heal, to serve, and to begin the process of transforming both for myself and for those that I come in contact with.

As part of my mission, I founded The Chopra Center. My mission: to educate health professionals, patients, and the general public on the connection between the

Wake up... Live the Life You Love,

relationship of mind, body, and spirit and healing. I teach people how to find their inner-self (most people have lost touch with theirs). When we find our inner-self, we find the wisdom that our bodies can be wonderful pharmacies—creating wonderful drugs—you name it, the human body can make it in the right dose, at the right time, for the right organ without side effects.

The body is a network of communication. Our thoughts influence everything that happens in our body. The problem is, many people automatically assume, "All I have to do is think positively, and everything will be fine." Because many assume this, they become unnatural and pretend everything is okay.

One must go beyond that; one must experience silence. It is when one experiences silence that healing energies become involved and a balance is created. Psalms 46:10 says, "Be still and know that I am God." When the body is silent, it knows how to repair itself.

Pursuing my mission gives me fulfillment. It makes me whole. It makes me feel that I will continue to do what I have been doing. If I had all the time and money in the world, this is I what I would choose to do. It gives me joy and a connection to the creative bar of the universe. I have realized that the pursuit of my goals is the progressive expansion of happiness. Pursue your goals and find your happiness, wholeness, and balance in this world.

Deepak Chopra

On The Enlightened Path

Sing Your Own Song
Dede Morse

"You're responsible for your own happiness. Live your dream." I'd heard those phrases countless times, but what did they mean?

I'd struggled for years to find out how to be responsible for my own happiness and how to live my dream. It always seemed to come up short. I was a clinical psychologist; a divorced mother with three sons. **Responsibility** was my middle name!

Lurking in the background was my first love—music. It kept poking through the fabric of my life since I sang for my first ice cream cone, at age three. In college, at UCLA, I majored in French, but minored in music. I was in the musical theater, the opera workshop, and Roger Wagner's chorale. Then my music hit a snag…graduation. I couldn't afford to pursue music any longer. I needed to work. I took a job as a flight attendant.

I lived in Los Angeles, New York City, Boston, and Kansas City. While in Manhattan, I flew to Europe. At 21, I thought I'd arrived. Seeing Rome, Madrid, London, Lisbon, and Frankfurt was certainly a childhood dream.

Four years later, I married. We had three children and my moving around continued because my husband worked for the airlines, too. Ten years passed. I began to sing again. I studied seriously and began performing in musicals. I was on my way! Then disappointment came.

Wake up... Live the Life You Love,

My coach disappeared. He had problems of his own. The theater group he'd formed fell apart and we dispersed. I continued to sing in chorals over the years, but I envied the soloists.

The urge to sing continued to exert itself. By the time I returned to California, my sons were grown and my psychology practice was thriving. There were plenty of opportunities to join groups, but I didn't want that. I wanted to be a soloist. By coincidence (or divine intervention), I attended a program at my church in which a four-person ensemble told the Easter story through song. I met the cast and learned that the organizers offered a course called "Finding Your Voice." I took the course and eight weeks later, sang my first solo in fifteen years—"Memory" from the musical *CATS*. I continue to study and sing wherever I can—parties, restaurants, churches, corporate events, charities, and even *The National Anthem* at sporting events. I have no doubt that I'm being guided.

Now, when I should be thinking about retirement, I am singing! I have a formidable team—a superb coach, a dynamic agent, and a perfectionist producer. I'm completing my first CD, a collection of jazz classics.

When I sing, I feel I'm conversing with God. He knows what I feel in all my various moods and lets me express myself. I may be joyous, tearful, content, or funny. They're all a part of me that I wish to share as a part of my humanity. Singing for an audience is the goal. It's not enough to sing for myself no matter how glorious it sounds to me. There must be an audience, an interaction between them and me. It's like a gesture of giving, which means nothing if there is no recipient.

On The Enlightened Path

I believe I put into song what the audience feels, the emotions they are not expressing. The closer I get to vibrating with them, the more satisfying the performance is for both of us. That's why music has universal appeal. Its expression is from the heart.

I'm happy. I feel that my professional goal—to relieve suffering—has been met. Now, I can feel and give joy through music. The moral of this story is to never give up following your dreams. There may be detours along the way, but if God has a plan for you, <u>get out of the way</u> and let Him lead. As I've discovered, no plan of mine could begin to equal His.

℃Dede Morse

Wake up... Live the Life You Love,

On The Enlightened Path

Life's Greatest Secret
Dave O'Connor

"*T*ony, do you think I could ever tap into those higher levels of consciousness like Gandhi, Buddha, or even Jesus?" I asked excitedly. I was 23 years old and had been practicing meditation for nearly 10 years.

My mentor looked over my head and answered, "I can see by your aura that the potential is certainly there but, I can also see that your vibrations would have to be a lot better."

"Auras? Vibrations? What do you mean?" I asked.

"Well everything is energy; we are all energy bodies vibrating at different rates. An aura is the energy field surrounding all things. Anybody who really looks at someone without their thoughts can see it. You can tell by the colors in the aura at what level a person is and how far they are on their spiritual path. The aura of Jesus was white and gold; these are the best colors to have. Black and brown are the worst."

"What are vibrations?" I asked, enthralled.

"Vibrations are streams of energy that run up and down in front of people," he said. "You can tell by looking at someone's vibrations if they are happy or depressed, healthy or sick, successful or struggling. At times you can even see their future. The average person is disconnected from their spirit because they are trapped in their negative thoughts. This prevents them from evolving spiritually.

Wake up... Live the Life You Love,

We live in a thought world that is nothing like reality—
reality is heaven-like, it is perfect."

I thought to myself, "So Obi-Wan Kenobi in *Star Wars*
was right when he said, 'the force is an energy field created by all living things—it surrounds us, it penetrates us, it
binds the galaxy together.' Yoda nailed it when he said to
Luke, 'Luminous beings are we—not this crude matter'."

So began my real training toward enlightenment. I
learned to relax my mind to such a level that I began to
get direction from my spirit. It showed me my future,
what I realized was my destiny. I was shown times long
ago, where levitation, telepathy, and clairvoyance were
normal. It was obvious to me that we were so much more
evolved back then because we had not yet lost our connection to our spirit or to God.

Over the years I have learned many of life's great
secrets. Perhaps the greatest of all is this: The vast majority of people fail in life because they think way too small.
People think small because they are full of self-doubt, and
are therefore double-minded. Access to the unlimited creative power within is granted only when you have a very
big goal that makes you single-minded. Your goal must
be so exciting, life-transforming, and powerful that it fills
you with passion, drive, enthusiasm, and certainty so that
whenever negative thoughts come up, just thinking of
your big goal wipes them out. That's why Jesus said, "If
you can believe and do not doubt in your heart, it will be
done for you."

Research from a new scientific success system known as
EDUCO™ reveals that all of the superachievers throughout time succeeded because they had a huge goal that
defied logic and they were extraordinarily single-minded.

On The Enlightened Path

This is the secret to all success. Your success can become unlimited and immortal by showing others the way. Whenever someone admires your success, tell them how you achieved it. Explain the big goal concept, but only on the condition that they also pass it on to others. In this way the whole world benefits from your success. Like an amazing wave that keeps going out, you can help millions of people. You will draw the same power into your life that sustained the spiritual masters, great inventors, and history-changers of our world. You will be making a vital difference in the world and will have a different kind of security and peace of mind.

Now, at the age of 37, I work with a team of like-minded people who are trained in this new EDUCO™ system, the only scientifically proven success system in the world today. Educo is simply a Latin word meaning to draw out from within. My team and I travel the world teaching people how to design the life of their dreams. Our aim is to put this creative pattern into the hands of every man, woman, and child on the planet. So please immortalize and spiritualize whatever success you achieve by inspiring others to do the same.

The world needs all of us to be fully evolved spiritually as we move into the Golden Age.

 භ Dave O'Connor

Wake up... Live the Life You Love,

Listen To Your Dreams
Carolyn P. Reynolds

On March 2, 1987, I awoke at 3:10 a.m. and bolted out of bed. I had heard a voice in my dream that said, "Color, shape, and form are very important to you and will be involved in your future work. You are, basically, an artist." I immediately wrote down the message, as I knew it was important.

We all receive guidance in different ways. Normally I feel things, see things, or just "know" things somehow, but this was the first time that I actually heard something. It was a commanding voice that engraved those words deep into my brain/spirit, never to be forgotten again. Me, an artist? Was God joking? I had two degrees in nutrition and worked in the medical field! What was I suppose to do? What did it mean?

Months passed before I was able to do anything with the information. I started taking some art classes at night, at a local community college. Drawing, water colors, ceramics—I was horrified with how bad I was. I remember I made 22 art objects in the ceramics class and pitched 21 of them at the end of the semester! Was God having fun at my expense? What was I suppose to learn?

Several years went by before I tried anything else. Then in 1995, I studied faux finishing, an art form that incorporates various interior decorative painting techniques.

Wake up... Live the Life You Love,

This time I surprised myself; I was quite good! And, it involved pure color, shape, and form! I loved it and was very happy. I then understood the meaning of the dream and had found my artistic expression. I would paint for the rest of my life!

To my surprise, a year later I encountered Feng Shui, an ancient body of knowledge that uses, among other things, colors, shapes, and forms to enhance, beautify, and harmonize environments. I fell in love with Feng Shui and soon realized that I had been practicing it all my life—I just didn't know it. I proceeded to study with several teachers from various traditions, to get a broader view of this wonderful healing art. I then had two sets of skills that reflected my dream. I became a certified Feng Shui Consultant/Decorative Artist, and I developed a style of my own over the next few years as I went about helping people.

One day a friend said to me, "Food also displays color, shape, and form." I had not yet made that connection, but she was right. Now, I had three complementary skills and they all involved healing—of the body/mind, the spirit, and the environment. I could help people integrate various aspects of their lives, starting with good nutrition and expanding to create healthy, balanced, colorful, unique environments, both at home and at work. It was exciting—everything starts with personal health or Chi. When we live in an orderly, beautiful, and sacred space, we are happier, feel better, and are more prosperous.

Since then I've also done "Staging" for Real Estate sales and helped plan a few gardens. I've also given many talks on Feng Shui at schools, organizations, homes, etc. I'm currently enhancing my talents by studying graphic

design. I can't even imagine at this point what I'll be able to create someday using technology. It's been a wonderful adventure, and, who knows what other skills might still develop?

Out of a dream came a new profession. That dream changed my life. Follow your dreams and see where they take you—and have a wonderful life in the process.

ೞCarolyn P. Reynolds

Wake up... Live the Life You Love,

On The Enlightened Path

My Journey Toward Enlightenment... from Modeling to Ministry
Dr. Mina J. Sirovy

*M*y life's journey seems to have evolved physically, then mentally, then spiritually; one could say "outside-in." In the initial physical phase I excelled in swimming and became a lifeguard instructor. By the second year of college I was burnt out from over-studying and wanted to have fun, so I left for New York City and the John Powers Modeling Agency. They promised me I'd be able to support myself within three months, but I was homesick.

Having been a small-town gal, I wanted a simpler life so I married my high school sweetheart and was happy as an Air Force wife and mother as long as I could model on the side. It was a glamorous distraction and I enjoyed being admired physically. In my 30's, I taught modeling but secretly encouraged my students to get beyond the superficial by enrolling in college. (Subconsciously I wanted to go back to finish college).

By that time I had learned the three "B's"—bowling, bridge, and buying—in order to be a good Air Force wife, but I was bored. What I really wanted was to get a degree in psychology. I had discovered that I had a natural ability to counsel and listen to wives whose husbands had died in Vietnam. Somehow I couldn't communicate my truth, that this was my life's mission to help others. This motiva-

Wake up... Live the Life You Love,

tional thrust moved me out of my marriage and my two girls and me into poverty. Getting an education, working, and raising daughters <u>almost</u> convinced me that I couldn't have it all.

My late 30's brought much soul-searching, and I became a transcendental mediator to gain peace of mind. Meditating twice daily produced a major shift in my way of thinking. Clarity of mind made advanced graduate work easier, so by age 50, I had earned my Ph.D. in psychology. I began teaching and opened a private practice in psychotherapy, which was very fulfilling. Soon, however, it became imperative that I be one of the cutting-edge therapists who was to put the soul (psyche) back into psychology. Successful therapy couldn't be confined to the mind, much less the brain. Honoring the Christ (light) within everyone needed to be included along with helping clients find their full potential.

I began studying metaphysics at an accredited school in California because I felt that developing my psychic/spiritual ability would enhance my counseling. If I could see clients' auras (colored electromagnetic fields surrounding them) I could tune into their deeper dimensions. After six years I became an ordained minister/spiritual healer. This training came just in time for me to heal myself as well as others. I had contracted a rare form of hepatitis for which there was no medical help, according to my liver specialist. He said that I would die unless I could have a liver transplant. Inwardly I said, "That's not the truth for me!" I knew after reading Deepak Chopra's *Perfect Health* that the liver can regenerate itself within six months. With the help of an herbalist and an acupuncturist, I visualized my liver back to health in four years.

On The Enlightened Path

Two years after complete recovery from liver disease, I was diagnosed with breast cancer. It was detected early and I used meditation, energy balancing, (EMF-B), and visualization to confine the cancer before my lumpectomy was performed. No chemotherapy or radiation was required. I now work with clients who are terminally ill.

Today I am a healthy 70-year-old. I have a Higher Source of healing power within me. I try to balance my sedentary life with gym workouts (back to the body). Before meditation I fill myself with light from my God connection. This gives me a warm, bubbly feeling, as though all my cells are coming to life. With clients I share this healing light by radiating front to back, top to bottom, and side to side. This glow has been validated by psychics.

Last Easter during meditation I felt as though I'd been struck by lightning—an old childhood fear. This so-called electrocution could be enlightenment (in-light-in-meant). Since this transformation I have been able to communicate with my granddaughter, Carly Jo, who lived only one day in November 2004. At the end of my meditations when my eyes are still closed, she speaks to me in word pictures such as a jet stream in the sky tracing a heart or a baby hand reaching out to me.

I continue on my spiritual path, knowing that everything is in Divine Order. I'm not retiring—only refiring!

℘Dr. Mina J. Sirovy

For your free gift, go to: **www.wakeupand.com**

Wake up... Live the Life You Love,

On The Enlightened Path

My Enlightened Path
Colin Smith

A panic attack prompted me to begin my enlightened path. It released me from over eleven years of unexpressed anger, anxiety, and depression. This eleven-year experience was a blessing in disguise, for it is in the valleys that we grow. I sought psychological support, and the series of healing programs released me from my preconceived ideas of myself and others. My vanity quickly disappeared and it was replaced by self-love. I then saw myself and the world at large through a new set of lenses.

I joined Toastmasters two years previous to the panic attack, to learn to feel better about myself. Then I received an urge to write. My first writing compared our lives to a fishing trip. On a fishing trip, we like to go with a good mate. When I go fishing, I go with my Good Mate, Jesus. In the quieter moments on my fishing trip, when there is a chance for a yarn, Jesus tells me that I need to learn to relax to overcome my long-held habit of anxiety.

After that story, I wrote and published a Christmas story, in comic pictorial form, about Santa Claus being introduced to the Holy Bible by a child in a shopping center. It is a story that comments on commercialism and materialism. Within two years of publishing this booklet, I was asked to play Santa Claus in a shopping center, just

Wake up... Live the Life You Love,

prior to Christmas. I did this for four years, before moving on.

At The International Permaculture Conference, 1996, in Perth, Western Australia, I met the author of the book, *The Children's Food Forests—An Outdoor Classroom.* When I ordered a copy, I put a couple of climbing bean seeds in the envelope. The author planted those seeds and the plants grew and bore such a wonderful crop that she asked me to become Mr. Beanseed in the children's pages of *The Permaculture International Journal.*

Children wrote to me for seeds and planting information. A Permaculture Group in Ghana, West Africa, wrote asking for vegetable planting seeds for their projects. I sent them the seeds and some books. A few months later, a local couple went on holiday to Ghana. While there, they went to visit my contact. When they knocked on his office door, he was reading *The Seed Savers Handbook,* the very book I had sent to him a few months earlier.

As a Landcare member, I initiated a campaign to advise other Landcare members and primary producers of the benefits of marketing their produce cooperatively. These primary producer cooperatives allow producers to maximize their returns, and to be better stewards of the land.

From a website, I conducted an Australia-wide petition to extend container deposit legislation to all of Australia. (It is a refundable deposit on the drink containers that litter our roads and highways: South Australia has had it since 1976.) The Australian Broadcasting Corporation interviewed me live on radio twice. During the second interview, they also included Mr. Ian Kiernan, AO, Chairman of "Clean Up Australia," who supports Container Deposit Legislation for all of Australia.

On The Enlightened Path

I am now designing an eBook, entitled *Why Kangaroos—and Other Dumb Animals—Don't Need a Health Care Scheme.* I use animals to give the messages. I use humor to strike at the indoctrinated system of stabilizing a person's health issues by masking the symptoms rather than identifying the underlying problems to eliminate them. Extreme bad health and poor statistics are the result of this approach. My goal is to be a catalyst for the change to natural health. I intend to establish a membership website called "Your Health Naturally."

Joining the *Wake Up...Live the Life You Love* family to become a co-author in the *Giving Gratitude* book has been the most exciting moment of my life. Being offered the opportunity to co-author in *The Enlightened Path* has reinforced that joy. Find your path, and walk it in service to others; you will love the journey.

ℰ∽Colin Smith

Wake up... Live the Life You Love,

On The Enlightened Path

The Voice of Beauty
Deborah Striker

Deep within the human soul, the voice of beauty stirs. In a world full of "bigger, better, and faster," our souls crave that unique moment when everything stops and only beauty exists. I have been blessed to share those moments with others and live my life in them by creating inspired works of art in stained glass for more than 5 years.

The path to these moments has been treacherous, at some points, and amazingly joyful at others. Every day holds adventures yet to be discovered—some I would have preferred not to take if given the option. I know now that each one that seemed difficult in the beginning had a deep, meaningful lesson to teach. An example? One of the most profound moments was when my husband was diagnosed with leukemia in September 2004. Through the immense outpouring of love, support, and healing energy along with traditional medical care, he is now in full remission and doing well. As a couple, it gave us a chance to truly focus on what we loved about our lives, as well as the parts that weren't working. It amazes me how many things seem unimportant when you're sitting in a hospital room holding the hand of a loved one while he endures chemotherapy. I know it has become cliché to say that a life-threatening illness changes your perspective but it is true. There really are no words to

Wake up... Live the Life You Love,

describe what kind of effect it has, and it is my sincere hope that you will not have to experience it personally.

Walking an enlightened path is not always easy. It comes with an understanding that the universe and all of humanity are connected and depend on each other for kindness and compassion. You must be able to step outside yourself and know that the tough times are just a small part of the entire beautiful picture. Change will come. If we are open to it and accept it happily, it tends to come more gently. When we are too rigid and refuse to change, the universe seems to find a way to get its point across anyway.

Like the myriad colors in a wonderfully wrought piece of stained glass, all of humanity reflects individual gifts and talents which create a beautiful world. The rewards of living your path are reaped not only in your <u>own</u> life, but also in the lives of everyone you meet. What does your soul crave? What do your hands desire to create? Find your personal path and live it!

May your steps be blessed!

ొDeborah Striker

How I Found My Enlightened Path
Jodi M. Valdes

*O*n August 8, 2004, I had a dream that would forever change my life. I can say that I spiritually "awoke" on that day. I received a message from my soul. That night, as I was dreaming, I was startled by a loud inner "popping" sound. The sound was different than anything I had ever heard. It was the kind of sound that, when you hear it, you know that it comes from your soul. The sound appeared to originate from the inside of my brain. It was almost as if my soul were talking to me.

Immediately after I experienced the "pop," I found myself floating bodiless in an open isolated foggy space. The silent fog-filled space stretched for endless miles in every direction. My inner consciousness was transported to this space. There was no sense of temperature, boundaries, or time. I felt as if I was transported to the very mystical place of my inner spirit. I existed only in the company of my own thoughts. "I must be dead," I thought. What happened next shed enlightenment on my life's meaning.

There I was, floating, and an overwhelming realization hit me like ton of bricks. "When you die, all you have is the sum of your past experiences!" Feelings and thoughts of my life accomplishments reeled past my mind's eye as though I were watching a movie in fast forward. Wow! I had wasted a lot of my life watching rerun television

Wake up... Live the Life You Love,

shows, working at jobs I did not like, and simply existing without meaning or purpose.

This dream symbolized a near-death experience. It saved my life. When I awoke from the dream I was a changed person. Today I feel more in tune with energy vibrations in the environment around me; I understand that each action I take affects my future. I have a sense of purpose and urgency. I have more patience and an increased sense of forgiveness and understanding toward others. Each of us is walking through our own life lessons to experience and grow from them.

Understanding this realization gives me strength when I am facing life's challenges. This dream symbolized the end of my old life and the beginning of my new life. I had let myself become a paperweight in my own office. My work had become a habit; I had lost the meaning of why I was called to work in my chosen field of social service. Today I feel a new sense of inner peace and passion for life. I am driven to better myself each day by living the life I love.

Here are five secrets I learned from my dream:

- Learn from crisis in your life. Crisis could bring unexpected gifts of growth. Your life is a classroom to learn about the true self within you.
- Pay attention to coincidences. They happen for a reason and offer hidden blessings. The mystery of the universe operates in harmony and synchronicity with events around us.
- Construct your life and take action. The universe is willing to give you what you ask for. First, create the thought of what you want and then ask the universe to bring it to you.

On The Enlightened Path

- Listen to your intuition. Your inner self is talking to you. Practice turning off the television once in a while to sit in silence. Listen to inner messages from your soul.

- All you have when you pass away is the history of your own thoughts. Therefore, take every opportunity to manifest positive thoughts, which in turn give out positive vibrations that lead toward an enlightened path.

∽Jodi M. Valdes

Wake up... Live the Life You Love,

The Enlightened ABC's
Christian Wasinger

When we were little we learned the ABC's; as we grow older we enjoy all the benefits of having these skills. Evolving into spiritual beings on an enlightened path, many of us feel the need to learn a new set of ABC's that helps us deal with life's challenges. I would like to share with you the first few letters of my "Enlightened ABC's" to help you on your path.

Always

We are always in control of our own thoughts and feelings. Remember Eleanor Roosevelt's famous quote: "Nobody can make you feel inferior without your consent." Every feeling starts with a thought. We cannot have feelings without thoughts. Thoughts are always constructed by words, so ultimately every feeling starts with a word. Words become thoughts and thoughts become feelings. In the end feelings are simply words and thoughts traveling through our bodies. And both words and thoughts can be changed!

Even feelings of fear, doubt, low self-esteem, anger, or hatred originated from words that you thought or spoke. Every word we think or speak has an effect on our nervous system and how we feel. By consciously changing the way we speak, we ultimately will change the way we feel. In order to achieve and maintain the changes we desire in life we must "clean up" our language.

Wake up... Live the Life You Love,

Blame

Many of us have experienced pain, hurt, and disappointment. Often these feelings are still very present many years after the occurring event, and some of us may still punish ourselves for what has happened. No matter what happened to us or how disappointing our past may appear, blame does not move us past these experiences to a more peaceful place. Blame uses a lot of our energy that could be used in more positive ways. As long as we keep blaming, whether we blame circumstances, ourselves, or others, we cannot move on to experience a peaceful fulfilled life. We cannot change what happened to us in the past; however, we can change how we now feel about the past. Forgive yourself and others, and you will be in a happier, more fulfilled place.

Choice

Choice is like a best friend—it's always there. At any given moment we have a choice. If one thing/thought/feeling exists that presupposes that, its opposite also exists. Whether we think we can or we think we cannot, we are right. The choice is ours. Where we are in life today is a direct result of the choices we made in the past. Rather than blaming ourselves for the choices we made, let's remind ourselves that we are always in control and that we can make different choices now.

Dream

When we were children we loved to daydream and pretend. We had dreams to be an astronaut, a movie star, a singer. We had all those wonderful dreams until we were repeatedly told, "stop daydreaming," "get real," "you can't," and "no." Hearing these powerful words over and over slowly, but surely, crushed those dreams and we

On The Enlightened Path

settled for an alternative that may not even have been second best. If that happened to you, I invite you to start daydreaming again. Use your imagination because we know that imagination, together with language and emotion, is the most powerful way to program the subconscious mind. After all, there are astronauts, movie stars, and singers out there today; the only difference is that they kept daydreaming until it became real.

Eliminate

Eliminate the obstacles and people from your life that do not support you or your dreams. When people belittle your dreams and ambitions it is often because of their own limiting beliefs, jealousy, or the regret that they let go of their own dreams. People don't like change if it pushes them out of their comfort zone. Changing and pursuing your dreams mean that the relationships in your life will change. Are the people in your life ready for that change? Are they on your support team? Surround yourself only with people who support and encourage you and your dreams.

Failure

Failure is feedback from the universe that helps us to assess our next steps in reaching our goals and dreams. Failure simply means that what we are doing is not quite perfected yet, and we need to change our course of action. Think about it! Anything you ever wanted in your life you always achieved. Sometimes you needed several tries and you kept changing your approach until that dream became reality. Other times failure can mean that your dream simply was not important enough or that your priorities have changed and you no longer choose to pursue this dream. Ultimately, there is no need to look at failure

Wake up... Live the Life You Love,

as a negative thing. You could even eliminate the word from your vocabulary. Trust me, you won't miss it!

Once you start applying these first few letters of my enlightened ABC's you will notice your life changing in the most positive ways. Please look for my upcoming book, which will be not only an enlightened ABC's but also an enlightened dictionary.

ଓଓChristian Wasinger

On The Enlightened Path

My Calling to be an Awakening Celebrant
Bruce Winkle

I have been very blessed to have horses in most of my life. Over the past 8 years I have been sharing energy work with them and have created "Energetic Wellness for Horses" classes to share this wonderful healing with horse lovers.

In the summer of 2004, I started receiving guidance from various sources that I would soon be sharing a new session with horses. I was sure it was going to be an advanced energy technique and was looking forward to its arrival.

During the Thanksgiving weekend, I was asked to perform a special Healers Attunement for a friend's horse named Dance. Dance had conveyed through an animal communicator that he wished to be a healer for all the transient horses that came through his barn. Since I was his owners' teacher I was honored. I derived an outline for the ceremony.

It was a very powerful ceremony including drumming, chanting, and various energy connections. Afterward, I wrote down all that had taken place thinking that this might be the new session I was called to do for horses. I was not sure whether this kind of ceremony would be widely accepted, but I would be happy to share whenever the opportunity arose.

For your free gift, go to: **www.wakeupand.com**

Wake up... Live the Life You Love,

In December, I went to do a follow-up energy session with another horse client named Smokey. Smokey's owner is also a student of mine, so I asked her to join in the assessment of Smokey's energy before I began his session. As I was scanning his energy systems, Smokey came over to me and stood face to face. He carefully and very gently put his muzzle up to my nose. He was very respectful of me but had a clear intention of where he needed to be. As he stood in this waiting position, I heard the words, "You have something for me." My mind was racing trying to guess what I had for him. Was it the Healer ceremony I had performed a couple of weeks earlier or was it something else. Then the word "Breath" came to me. Breath; the medium upon which the Spirit travels.

Taking in a deep breath, I began to blow softly into Smokey's right nostril. He stayed nose to nose, so I blew softly into his left nostril. The next breath flowed over Smokey's nose and went up his face. He stood transfixed. Then he slowly turned his head around and gave his owner a long look. He then turned back and brought his muzzle as close to my face as possible without touching. I began to send several breaths toward each of his chakras. The sound of softly blowing breath changed and became the sound of the wind as it blows across a vast prairie. As I continued, the wind noise intensified and a whistle sound intermittently joined it. Smokey began to quiver all over.

At one point Smokey went over to the stall door and gazed out as if seeing far away places and long ago events. He turned and again gave his owner a long, puzzled look before returning to absorb more of the whistling wind. When I completed the breath to each of his chakras, he

again returned to the stall door and gazed into far away places. As he stood at the stall door, he began to change. He became restless, agitated, and impatient. He pawed, snorted, spun, half-reared, and trotted in place with exaggerated elevation. He turned into a powerful, magnificent creature that needed to run free.

His owner became concerned that he was misbehaving and closed the stall door to keep him contained. I told her that it was all right. Smokey couldn't help it. I reconnected to his energy and he began to settle slowly and began the sighs, licking, and chewing he normally exhibited during an energy session. However, as soon as I released his energy he became agitated and wanted out of that stall. I suggested that we honor his wish.

I asked his owner to look into his eyes and share with me what she saw. She went and stood in front of Smokey. The eyes gazing back at her were solemn and dark and they seemed endlessly deep. It seemed as though he was seeing far into the distance and was remembering. I explained to the owner that this new session was just developing in me and that Smokey was the horse that had brought it forth. We were both greatly humbled by the experience.

As the full understanding of this event unfolded over the days that followed, it became clear why it was time for this special Horse Awakening ceremony. It is well known that horses are wonderful heart-centered beings and are here to be our special companions and teachers. When much of mankind forgot and treated them with much harshness, the horse had to separate from their true full power to remain in such unharmonious relationships. Now, many owners are reestablishing the true relationship

Wake up... Live the Life You Love,

with their horses and it is time to reunite the horses with their full power, bringing forth healing for all.

I am honored to share in these wonderful ceremonies and watch as each horse and owner begin their new journey together. To read more horse stories please visit my website.

ᏬBruce Winkle

A Blessing in Disguise
Sharon Shohreh Javdan

Through the tears that welled in my eyes, I made out the words "Help Wanted" reflected in the window. There was no way I could have handled even a job like that. I couldn't concentrate and my memory was quite foggy. My eating and sleeping patterns were completely out of whack. How could this be? Just a few weeks before that, I had a professional teaching job. I was creative and pretty good at it, if I may say so. Then, I was knocked off my path as surely as if I had been struck with a brick.

Kay was a co-worker, a tall thin blonde. She was working on getting the same Master's degree that I already had. Through our brief conversations I found that she was having a hard time finishing her degree. She knew that I had done very well in school and she seemed bothered by that. After all, I was a foreigner! How could I have done better in school than she? I wondered if it was my accent that made her doubt my skills. I started doubting myself. Was my English good enough? Then came that ugly day! We were in the office talking about our students and Kay said, "All the Middle Eastern students cheat!" She then looked at me briefly. I was born in the Middle East. Perhaps she said that because she was jealous of me, or perhaps she was prejudiced. Did the other co-workers see me in the same way? Now, I was prejudiced.

Wake up... Live the Life You Love,

In the weeks to come, there was a mysterious air around the office; many awkward, silent moments, whispers behind the short walls, unexplained looks or inside jokes exchanged among some teachers. I felt left out. Were they talking about me? I felt guilty even thinking that. I felt a little crazy. It was hard to form a clear reality. I reached out to my husband but he wasn't able to help. When I asked Kay about her comment on the Middle Eastern students, she would deny that it had anything to do with me. Yet my heart knew better. I couldn't work there any longer; I was too depressed. The incident of prejudice wasn't the only reason for my depression, but it did push me over the edge.

I was faced with two choices: to sit and wallow in my own grief, or to see this as a blessing in disguise and find a lesson in it all. Having been exposed to a small dose of prejudice, I became more and more aware of prejudices in our society and their impact on everyone. I say "everyone" because, although historically there are the oppressors and the oppressed, prejudice affects all people negatively and everyone is a victim.

My family believes in "oneness of humanity." I felt an urge to learn more about cross-cultural and race relations in this country. I started sharing my new-found knowledge and insights by giving talks on the subject. I developed a variety of workshops for reducing prejudice. For a few years I continued to offer my presentations as a community service. Then people started asking me how much I charged! I realized that to do more of this work, I should do it professionally and get paid. In 1990, I established "A New Human Race," a consulting firm that promotes recognition of oneness of humanity and valuing

On The Enlightened Path

diversity through presentations, workshops, seminars, and products.

Although it was painful at the time, I am glad I found my calling, my life's purpose. I hope you will find yours, wherever it lies. Don't forget to look for it among life's disguised blessings. That is how I was led to my enlightened path.

                                        ☙Sharon Shohreh Javdan

Wake up... Live the Life You Love,

On The Enlightened Path

You Can Harness Your Stress
Christina Reynolds Goncalves

Stress can be a very useful form of energy if we know how to take full advantage of it. People rarely realize that even before the levels of stress at home or at work create psychosomatic disorders in us, we can learn to "read" our reactions and feelings in time to actually avoid sickness. There is always something constructive to be learned from symptoms and body language, even after we have started feeling ill, and sometimes the process can also be reversed.

Once my daughter called me from summer camp, sobbing because she didn't want to take the antibiotics she knew they'd give her for the sore throat she had developed. It was nighttime and they were going to take her to town the next day to see a doctor. I tried to console her by explaining that even though she was well aware of the incredibly swift and profound effect of a dose of her constitutional remedy (she'll never forget the earache that subsided within minutes, after one dose!), she could take the antibiotics without necessarily going through the adverse effects they usually brought on, as long as she wasn't using them to make her body "shut up." If she could understand what her throat was trying to "tell" her, she would grow from the experience, which was more important than avoiding the antibiotics. She later told me they never had to take her to the doctor, for as soon as

she realized the whole situation was an unconscious reaction to feeling cornered into singing in public, she began to face her shyness and to heal!

As a physician, having worked with Classical Homeopathy in Brazil for more than 20 years, experience has shown me that the inherently human trait of making conscious choices is the key to whole new levels of life quality. Life may "deal us a bad hand," but what we do with each experience is entirely up to us.

Classical Homeopathy can help a person deal with any level of stress as it manifests, whether physically or emotionally. An overly sensitive child may have nightmares; a woman may have PMS; anyone may have acid reflux or Irritable Bowel Syndrome or allergies. The appropriate constitutional remedy can give each individual a significant boost in his quest for new levels of health.

Allowing ourselves the flexibility to flow with changes, we notice that there is often more than one "right" way to do things and we realize the necessity of understanding other people's points of view. We can piece "reality" together like a jig-saw puzzle when we're free from the illusion that for one person to be right the other has to be wrong. This is literally a new paradigm and it frees us up to look at all angles of any situation, welcoming other inputs as we determine what is best for all involved.

Individual health issues benefit from an attitude free of prejudice and open to new ideas. Our bodies speak to us through body language, as our dreams speak to us in symbolic terms. Diseases themselves contain messages we can learn to understand. With these tools for a better quality of life comes the responsibility for making the necessary

On The Enlightened Path

changes in our attitudes and beliefs so that we may really grow and mature. In this way we can harness the stored energy of stress to wake up the potential that lies dormant in each one of us.

&Christina Reynolds Goncalves

Wake up... Live the Life You Love,

On The Enlightened Path

Our Perception Determines Our Experience
Gregory Scott Reid

Not long ago, I traveled back east to Ohio and Chicago, Illinois. While I was there, I was amazed that the friends I made along my journey seemed to have completely different observations of the states in which they lived. For example, when I asked what the winters were like there, I got completely opposite answers from people, depending on where they originally lived. When I asked the question of a former Californian, she talked as if she'd landed in Siberia, recounting the snowfall and treacherous conditions meant for only the wildest of beasts. When I asked the same question of a native resident, he painted a beautiful picture of the changing seasons, each more spectacular than the last, and recounted wonderful memories of having the good fortune to grow up in such a picturesque land. What's the difference here? Their perception dictated their experience.

It's like the old stories about a bank robbery. The event could have taken place in broad daylight, with 30 eyewitnesses, yet each could give a completely different account of what he or she saw happen. This can also happen when someone in your office or home says something to you, and you receive a different message than the person intended.

Why does this happen? I believe it's because our perception determines our experience.

Wake up... Live the Life You Love,

I'll bet at one time or another we've all gone into a grocery store and noticed that everyone seemed happy, helpful, and cheerful that day. Even the people in the checkout line were full of good spirits. Yet, when we've gone another day, we've had a completely different experience. We found people to be grumpy and in a bad mood—every one of them.

I believe we view our outside world the same way we see ourselves in our inside world. That's why many people continually attract drama into their lives while others do not, or why some people get into fights all the time while others refuse to let the same situation get the best of them.

It could be why, when we feel out of place and chaotic on the inside, we tend to attract more chaos and drama to our outside selves. If we feel anger and resentment on the inside, we will, in turn, attract it to our outer worlds as well.

With that said, let me ask you the following questions:

How has your outside world looked lately? Are the people around you happy and productive? Are they full of life and passion, or do you find yourself in your own little tornado that seems to constantly bring nothing by negative energy your way? In other words, does it seem that everyone around you has problems and can never catch a so-called "break?"

Remember, in life you have choices. You have the choice to work on your inner self, to create a brighter outer self. Have you ever seen someone who has lost some weight and noticed that they seem to have a new glow? Or looked into someone's eyes just after their first child was born? There's a spark there, right? Well, here's the

On The Enlightened Path

good news. You have the ability to re-spark yourself. In fact, here's a challenge: *Take notice.* I'm not asking you to do anything but become aware of how you're viewing things around you.

By doing so, you'll find that when you're at your happiest, everyone else around you in your outside world will be as well. On the flip side, if you want to know why the walls seems to be crashing in on you, look inside and see what's out of place, and then take action to repair it.

It's that simple. Because when it's all said and done, our perception really does determine our experience.

&Gregory Scott Reid

Wake up... Live the Life You Love,

On The Enlightened Path

Through the Tunnel of Life
Brandt Morgan

*I*n 1998, I had a near-death experience. The circumstances don't matter much now, except to say that my heart was in distress and I was lying under a tree, looking up at the stars and the moon through a canopy of leaves. My spiritual teacher, don Miguel Ruiz, who is also a medical doctor, was kneeling by my side.

"Close your eyes and take a deep breath," he said.

I closed my eyes and took a deep breath. Miguel pushed his thumbs against my eyeballs. In that moment, I found myself floating peacefully in the blackness of empty space. In the far distance I saw a tiny star—a pinprick of light that grew quickly larger and brighter. As the light approached, it exploded with life, radiating sparks brighter than the blaze from an acetylene torch.

In the next moment the sparks engulfed me, and I went blasting through a tunnel of light. The entire tunnel was composed of magnificent little spirits, each one sentient, intelligent, alive. Speeding past me like stars in hyperspace, each one knew and loved me intimately, and I knew and loved them back. Somehow I knew they were rushing out from the void to have experiences in the world—to become trees, rocks, people, mosquitoes, whales, wildflowers—and I was rushing back to merge with the source of all light.

Wake up... Live the Life You Love,

I was in utter ecstasy. "Oh, my God, Miguel!" I exclaimed. "Is this where you go?"

"Now you know what it is like to die," Miguel said matter of factly.

No, it can't be! I thought. *I've never felt more alive!* Like a drop of water that suddenly remembers it is part of the ocean, all I wanted to do was race down that pulsating river and merge with the unfathomable love at the other end.

Fortunately, Miguel did not buy my enthusiasm. "I'm talking with the archangels," he said firmly, "and they're telling me that if you go, you're not coming back!"

Reluctantly I returned, with a little help from Miguel. But after my journey I was never the same, and neither was my world. Colors were brighter, faces were more radiant. Life was more miraculous and inviting. The joy of consciousness emanated from everything—even from chairs, rocks, and refrigerators.

For weeks afterward, my heart felt like a glowing coal. I watched birds tumbling in the trees and felt their heartbeats as my own. I gazed into people's faces and saw myself as in a magic mirror. I listened to music and heard playful sparks of light singing messages of love and communion.

For months I tried to make sense of my experience. Years later, it is still a great mystery, but, repeatedly it tells me this: *The tunnel is not out there; it's inside. God is in every cell and every cell rejoices at the memory of its maker. We all came from the light, and we're all going back to it. In fact, we never left it. It's as present as the air we breathe.*

If that is true, then why not live it? Today my greatest joy is to show people how to access their own inner lights—through here-and-now, near-*life* experiences. Like

On The Enlightened Path

my mentor, don Miguel, I offer coaching, classes, journeys, books, and tools intended to help people find their true selves and live their greatest dreams. All these things are only signposts though, and all of them point to the same truth: *You are one with all that is, and you can create anything you want.* So don't miss it. Find your own inner light and let it shine. Discover your dream and live it, and don't regret or worry about a thing; the only moment that matters is now.

          ❧Brandt Morgan

Wake up... Live the Life You Love,

On The Enlightened Path

From Loser…to Leader…to Lover
Charles Hai Nguyen

*N*ot long ago I wrote an article in the *Wake Up Live Series*, titled "From Loser…to Leader…to Lover." It's an article about my success story and how I turned my life around and went from a loser in the eyes of friends and family, to a leader leading an insurance brokerage company to the next level. I went from being broke, struggling day by day, to developing unstoppable, financial momentum, with an abundance of opportunities available to me. Not only is my career on the path of success, my relationships with my wife, Nichole, my son, Tyler, and my daughter, Tia, have grown closer and stronger. What else can I ask for? I'm building wealth in business as well as in my home.

Although it was very liberating to have the confidence of knowing that I could accomplish whatever I set my mind upon, I still felt that something was missing inside. I kept asking myself, "How can I take my life to an even higher level of purpose and fulfillment?" The answer didn't come until several events took place in my life.

In the beginning of the year when we celebrated my dad's 66th birthday, dad and mom called a family meeting, consisting of four brothers, a sister, and our spouses. Dad announced that he was making peace with my mom after 6 months of dispute and that the family would be closer. Because of my parent's unhappy relationship, our

Wake up... Live the Life You Love,

family suffered. We hardly saw each other and barely spoke at occasions such as birthday parties and Christmas. After listening to my dad, we discussed our views. I poured my heart out, expressing my ideas about why things didn't work out and what we could do. I didn't point fingers at anyone but rather identified the events in the past that led us to be this way. I tried to give them a vision of how things could be and how we could get there by giving examples of things that had worked for me. I felt that everything I had learned, all the wisdom I had accumulated had led me to that day: to be able to lead my family to a better relationship. Several of my family members told me afterward, that that was a great talk I gave and that they were proud of me.

Months passed and I found that nothing had changed much. Some of the family still had not made any progress; they were still having the same issues. I felt frustrated and helpless so I set out on my mission to discover more solutions. I attended Tony Robbins' "Leadership Academy." My primary focus was, "How do I influence people who don't want to change?" I learned two key elements that I need to work on in order to further my skills to influence my loved ones. The first key was to commit to a standard of constant and never ending improvement. By doing so, I have reached a higher level of awareness and have acquired the skills to handle challenges and overcome obstacles. There must be an awareness that things need to change before change will occur. The second key element was that I need to be less prejudiced and more compassionate. I realized that I need to understand and appreciate the views of others. I need to learn and appreciate who they are, and what they want out of life.

On The Enlightened Path

Everyone sees the world differently. Through understanding their experiences, dreams, and desires, I can discover what really motivates and drives them. From there, I may guide them.

When I got home from the training, I shared my learning experience with Bruce Patrick, one of my clients. I also discussed the issues my family was facing and told him that I was hesitant to interfere in their lives. He told me that since I had harnessed the awareness, the wisdom, and the skills necessary to resolve these challenges, I was obligated to intervene and do the best I could. He pointed out that I was no longer an innocent bystander and that I couldn't just sit back and let things slide by. I had a responsibility to make the world a better place.

As an enlightened person, I have realized that I can't use the excuse that "I didn't know better." I know I need to follow my new path now and I have the responsibility to do whatever it takes to be on the journey. I know you are walking or, at least, you're starting your journey on the enlightened path. Because you have read this article and other articles in this book, you have raised your awareness and probably discovered some ideas about making the world a better place. You owe it to yourself and your loved ones to take the journey. You will realize, as I did, that taking on the journey won't be easy. Just have faith that you have all the necessary resources to overcome those challenges. As a result, you will grow to be more; to have more happiness, wealth, and success. You won't be alone; you will have your loved ones with you on the journey.

እ⁓Charles Hai Nguyen

Wake up... Live the Life You Love,

On The Enlightened Path

Guided by Divine Light
Laurelle Shanti Gaia

*T*he Infinite Light Healing Studies Center (Infinite Light) was born from a childhood experience. When I was 7, on summer vacation with my family, I was playing in the Atlantic Ocean in Florida. I was pushed under the water by a wave and was held under for what seemed to be eternity. Just as I began to panic, a strong male voice, which I heard clairaudiently, "inspired" me to breathe very gently and not draw the water into my lungs, but to simply "ask" the oxygen in the water to help me breathe. I did exactly that and immediately became calm and peaceful, floating in what seemed to be an ocean of light. Within this luminous sea I saw a great light growing clearer and stronger, and from this light a form appeared. I recognized this form to be Jesus, and he was surrounded by many spiritual beings, including Medicine Buddha, Mother Mary, and Kwan Yin.

As the light of Christ appeared clearer to me, from his heart area a bubble of light appeared. It was beautiful, shimmering and iridescent. The bubble dissolved slowly, and from it emerged a beautiful symbolic representation of the Christed Consciousness, the essence of enlightenment. I then heard this phrase:

> *Laurelle, Laurelle, Laurelle,*
> *remember, remember, remember.*
> *With this together we shall create peace .*

Wake up... Live the Life You Love,

In that moment, I found myself standing up, unharmed and very happy to be alive. I was also a bit bewildered because my name at birth was Laura Ellen, yet the name Laurelle stirred a remembrance deep within my being.

A year later, I decided it was time to become a responsible person. I thought, "Responsible people need a plan for their lives." So I began to wonder what I should do with my life. My grandmother had recently given me a *Bible*. She said, "Honey, if you ever have any questions about life, all the answers are in this book." I thought this was wonderful; I would just look in the *Bible*, find my name, and learn what I would do when I grew up. Much to my dismay I did not find my name.

As I diligently searched the *Bible* for the answer to my question, I became mesmerized by the stories of Jesus doing healing. I proudly announced to my family, "When I grow up, I am going to travel around the world, help heal people, and teach them that they can do this too." The response was, "That's very nice honey, but you can't do that; only Jesus can." "Oh no," I said confidently, "It says right here (in *John*), "These things I do you can do and even greater."" The response I received was, "I know that's what it says, but that's not what it means."

So, for various reasons, I allowed my inner knowing of my life's purpose to be blocked when I was just 8 years old. But not before I had a little conversation with God. I said "God, I really want to help people like Jesus did; they say I can't, but the *Bible* says I can. So I guess if I am supposed to do this you'll figure it out and show me someday."

On The Enlightened Path

That prayer was completely released and forgotten, but looking back, I was guided from that moment on. I was guided through good times and tough times. Sometimes I made the easy choice, and sometimes I made harder ones. But somehow, God helped me find my way to live the answer to the prayer of an 8-year-old with a dream. I didn't think much of those childhood experiences for many years, but then, powerful events in my life unfolded to teach me about energy and the fact that we are all spiritual beings, capable of radiating the full power of divine healing love and that we are truly limitless.

In 1994, Utumei, the symbolic representation of the Christed Consciousness, returned and I began to receive light and energetic messages containing certain vibrations and information. One of the messages told me that these were transmissions of Infinite Light.

I timidly began to share this information, as I was guided, with people I knew to be experienced with healing energies, prayer, and the power of positive thought. These transmissions ultimately became part of the teachings we share through the Infinite Light Healing Studies Center. To my humble and utter amazement, every person who allowed the essence of the transmissions into their personal lives or their healing work, reported beautiful experiences of healing, spiritual growth, and empowerment.

Many found that after exposure to and integration of these energies they became keenly aware of their personal "calling" in life. They awakened to their latent abilities as artists, musicians, composers, healers, effective parents, inspirational speakers, etc. Simply by allowing their

Wake up... Live the Life You Love,

own Infinite Light to awaken, people can remember their purpose.

It is from these experiences that the training programs, services, and products that I share through the Infinite Light Healing Studies Center have grown. For the past 16 years we have been helping people learn to heal themselves. I have traveled around the world teaching systems of spiritual healing. Today I live in Sedona, Arizona, one of the most magnificently beautiful and sacred places on the earth. I thank God for the many blessings and for the divine guidance I receive in my life every single day.

It is my sincere prayer that those who feel a heart connection to Infinite Light will allow it into their lives and that it will assist them in awakening, remembering, fully expressing, and being their divinity.

&Laurelle Shanti Gaia

Buttered Biscuits

Yolande Nicholson-Spears

I started my new life with seven changes of clothing, a sleeping bag, and an alarm clock in Hartford, Connecticut.

I was lucky. No, I was blessed! I was finally safe. And yet, just one year before, I wasn't sure whether I would or could escape the darkness I had concealed.

My so-called friends told me, "Just be patient." They were mistaken.

I learned than an unhealthy relationship rarely works itself out. I was on automatic denial. I woke up each day and gave myself a daily dose of excuses to remain imprisoned. I felt responsible to everyone except myself. How would I explain to my co-workers, friends, and family that I couldn't take it anymore? I was embarrassed and ashamed of my dark secret that I had concealed in this mockery of a so-called perfect marriage.

I had become accustomed to his random fits of anger. I had witnessed chairs being propelled into walls and an occasional forceful slap across my face because I was disobedient and provoked him. I continued to accept his excuses to justify his behavior. After all, we were college-educated and lived in a very nice house in a wonderful neighborhood, with two children in private school. This type of madness just does not happen to people like us.

Wake up... Live the Life You Love,

After these occasional "misunderstandings" he would plead "Honey, I am so sorry, I didn't mean it. I love you."

Finally, one Saturday morning, I had baked his favorite buttered biscuits and a veggie omelet. He entered the kitchen with a sour attitude. He was unhappy that he had not received a call about his appointment for a prestigious board position.

I tried to persuade him to stop dwelling on the negative. His anger escalated. Then he shoved all of the food onto the floor. Disgusted, I attempted to walk away. He sprang from his chair, grabbed me by the throat, yanked my head backward, and shoved me onto the floor. He grabbed my hair and began to pound my head against the cold tile floor! Struggling and screaming, I thrust my fingernails into his eyes and frantically kicked him off of me. He yelled, covering his wounded face, and released me as I sat motionless in the hallway.

After the buttered biscuits incident, I knew I had to escape or die! I silently planned my escape. I knew I needed the power of God and prayer to help me.

I began a ritual of reciting *Psalms 23* and *The Lord's Prayer* several times throughout the day. I recited a phrase my mother taught me, "This Lord or something better... let Thy will be done."

About ten months later, my employer offered me a transfer and promotion to New England. It was a miracle, and God's answer to my prayers! I left my new house, car, clothes, and everything from that marriage behind and I never looked back. I was finally free!

My painful nightmare had finally come to an end. I still thank God for giving me one more day! Now, twenty-five years later, I am married to my soul mate, Amir

On The Enlightened Path

Spears, and have two wonderful children, Rachel and Lanze.

Each day, I acknowledge that I am blessed to be alive and I cherish my job at The Bushnell Center for the Performing Arts. I am so fortunate to have a boss and mentor, Ronna Reynolds, who has given me the opportunity to be creative and live a life I love. Daily, I still recite *Psalms 23*. I know that the Creator will always deliver **me** and **you** out of the shadows of darkness, if we only believe that we can and will defeat our personal demons!

You too, can start today to map out a plan to Wake Up and Live the Life You Want and Love!

᎔Yolande Nicholson-Spears

Wake up... Live the Life You Love,

On The Enlightened Path

Path
Nasrin Salehi

I was born in a large Iranian family. Being rejected by my mother was the first experience of my life. This happened when I was only 4 months old. My mother was disappointed; she was expecting a boy. It really hurts; I had no way of expressing my feeling except crying and crying. Later, my mother changed her mind and decided to love me but I became a very sensitive child and carried my sensitivity and my feeling of being unloved and unworthy through my life for many years.

I did not know how to control those unwanted feelings, and they were running my life. I denied and suppressed them; I tried to run other people's lives as my instrument to control them, to be there for them, to solve their problems. It felt good because I felt needed; I could not stand to be alone.

It was too painful to deal with all the sadness. I blamed my mother, my family, my country, the government, the weather, and still felt those unwanted feelings.

Later in life I met Shahram and married him, and we moved to the United States. We decided to have a family, but I could not conceive because of a major medical condition. Even though the doctor told me I had only a five percent chance to get pregnant, I still held my hope. The same day, after I left the doctor's office, I went to walk on the beach. Along the way there was a small

Wake up... Live the Life You Love,

metaphysical book store. I was guided to visit the shop and bought some tapes on mediation, visualization, and healing. For the first time, I just trusted my inner voice. The next day I quit my job and started to do my home-work: praying, meditating, and visualizing.

After six months, I revisited my doctor. He was sur-prised and happy to announce that I was pregnant. Oh God! It was the most beautiful moment of my life. I trusted my intuition and it worked. During the next six months I decided to let go; I forgave all those who had hurt me, I surrendered and released everything to a higher power. I learned the meaning of loving detach-ment, developed empathy and I changed my attitude. I developed a deep awareness of myself, and others. I let go and opened up to the universal and spiritual principles. I reprogrammed my mind.

Giving birth to another being is the most precious gift of God. For me it was the turning point. It totally transformed me. I am so blessed to listen to my intu-ition; it took me to the higher state of consciousness. I allow the creator to work through me and lead me to the right place with the flowing energy of the universe. Now I know the light of truth radiates from a higher power and reveals the absence of sickness and limitation. By sur-rendering to the higher power, I started to get to know myself, and let go of my lower nature. All it took was to shift my consciousness from darkness to the light.

Through practice, I learned how to acknowledge my feeling and my thinking, yet staying detached from them; they are not who I am, they are only the instrument of my human experience. Every day I have a checklist that I go through, to examine my emotion, mind and body,

On The Enlightened Path

so I can create harmony. I honor myself by feeling selfless but worthy. I learned how to love myself unconditionally, and focus on my spiritual principles. Thirty years of gaining knowledge about human behavior did not help me as much as my decision to open my heart.

In the past, I rescued people and lived their lives; now I love to empower those beings of light that come on my path. As a teacher and a full time student, I share the oneness with all and remind them that they are the light of the world, they are co-creators, and can manifest anything they desire by finding their true identities. Life is like a running river with loads of adventures and obstacles on its path. If we know where we are going, to the ocean of love, joy, peace, harmony, and the kingdom of higher power, nothing may stop us.

We may pass from all human experience, overcome obstacles, because we know deep down it is only a short journey, our destiny is an ocean of unconditional love, and light which is our true nature, if we remember that even if we are a drop of that ocean, therefore, we have all the ingredients of the ocean of light inside us. All we need is to discover it within ourselves. At the present time, through workshops, private sessions, lecturing, and most of all being in my truth, spiritual dancing, the light of the Creator through me empowers the sisters and brothers of light by sharing the power of visualization, praying, and meditation to heal themselves in many levels and to claim their state of health which is true nature of all, so they can share the light with others. I love what I do and I do what I enjoy.

ℰ∋Nasrin Salehi

Wake up... Live the Life You Love,

On The Enlightened Path

The Path of Possibilities
Jacqueline Lynch

*I*t was 2002, the end of February and I had just arrived from a weekend trip visiting my friend and her family in Phoenix, Arizona. I felt pretty lousy and my ear was, once again, hurting. But I pulled myself together and attended a presentation of German short films at a hotel in Beverly Hills. I was not feeling well throughout the evening and was glad when I could leave and go to sleep. The next morning I woke up with a terrible earache. After taking a homeopathic remedy that my doctor had recommended, the pain became more intense and I thought my eardrum would burst. My brother brought me soup, but I could not eat. When I got out of bed, my left knee was wobbling and shaking uncontrollably. It took me another month to realize that this was an outbreak of Multiple Sclerosis, which I had been diagnosed with 12 years prior but had never experienced any physical difficulties until then.

I kept my illness a secret from my family until Mother's Day in May, when my Mom saw that I had difficulty walking. I had just started Nei Kung, a powerful system of Martial Art chi kung based on the fundamental principles of the inner flow of vital energy, or CHI. It has been utilized for centuries by the practitioners of Chinese med-

Wake up... Live the Life You Love,

icine and acupuncture. Meeting my instructor, Nei Kung James Borrelli was the first step into a different way of life for me. When I changed acupuncturists, I was met with resistance, but today I realize that it was a path that I had needed to take. The new acupuncturist began to make the "table turn" after a few months. He had never had anyone respond so well to the treatment. He told me that several factors were involved in my improvement.

My life turned around completely! I changed my nutrition and my attitude. I have regular acupuncture treatments and I practice Nei Kung and spirituality on a daily basis. My soul is being repaired and it's the most exciting experience I've ever had.

In June 2003 at 2 A.M., I awoke with water dripping on my face from the ceiling of my apartment. Today I believe this was God allowing me to discover an existing, dangerous, invisible mold in my apartment. For years I had been having ear and eye problems. I told my landlord that I couldn't put my finger on it, but that I knew something was wrong in the apartment or in the building. He didn't believe me, and still might not to this day. A mold inspection revealed that there was indeed mold. My blood test showed a fungus and a breathing test showed the beginning stages of asthma. I found a lawyer who would work on contingency. I gave it all to God and decided to allow Him to take care of it. I'm still doing footwork and supplying information, but this case should be coming to an end soon.

The anxiety that I had been feeling because of my lack of funds, has now turned to serenity and healing for me. I have learned that Health is Wealth and I hope soon to

On The Enlightened Path

be going down the path of recovery. My dream is to share with others that there is an alternative way of healing and that it is filled with possibilities.

ᴇᴏJacqueline Lynch

Wake up... Live the Life You Love,

On The Enlightened Path

The First Essence of Life,
"Our Body the Foundation"
Garry Choy

When you lose control of your body, nothing else in life matters, not work, not dreams, not friends, not even family. I had to learn the hard way that, when my body failed and I was in pain, I could not think of anything other than my body. I was in constant pain and discomfort.

Like any other kid, I grew up trying to follow the traditional dream of success: study hard, get good grades, get a great job and life would be "happily ever after." Well I did exactly that: I studied hard, graduated with an honors engineering degree, and joined an aerospace company. I flew around the world in business class and stayed at four star hotels. Life was wonderful. Everything seemed to be picture perfect. I was doing what I had studied for all my life and I was working harder than ever trying to impress my superiors.

After working for about one year I started to notice that my stomach did not feel right. I had this constant feeling of something heavy in my stomach as if I had swallowed a rock. Soon, I discovered that the only means to relieve this sensation for awhile was to eat. I found myself eating and munching on all sorts of foods and snacks. This worked for awhile but eventually I found that the sensation would not go away; it got worse. I was

Wake up... Live the Life You Love,

in constant pain and had difficulty thinking of anything else. That's when I decided to seek medical attention.

To my surprise the doctor informed me that I had a serious ulcer. This seemed strange, for I always thought that this sort of thing always happened "to the other guy"—not me. After all, no one in my family had ever had ulcers. The doctor also informed me that, if things got worse, it could become life threatening. After I heard that, "My life flashed before my eyes." I wondered what working so hard and being successful really meant if I was going to die. I decided that my job was not worth it and I would quit and travel instead and climb perhaps the mountains in Nepal. I had heard that is where people go to find themselves. A friend of my father heard of my plight and offered to introduce me to a famous Taoist Tai Chi teacher. He was also taking classes and had heard that it could help with a variety of medical conditions. I decided to try this eastern approach before giving up my career. I practiced what the teacher taught me six hours a day, almost seven days a week. Slowly the pain in my stomach faded away. After 3 months of study, the problems with my stomach had all but disappeared. I was well again and I felt that I was given a second chance at life. This time I would make the most of it. I vowed never to go through this experience again and to learn as much as I could from this teacher. Eventually I traveled the world and sought out my teacher's teacher and his colleagues in my quest for higher learning and understanding.

After 20 years of study, I now understand. People who take responsibilities seriously usually let the associated stresses affect their body. This is true whether these responsibilities regard relationships, family, work, or

On The Enlightened Path

finances. Unfortunately, this is all too common in our world. A reason our health is affected is because we don't feel good and have somehow lost the First Essence of Life, the ability to take control of our body and learn to let go when we are under stress or when things just don't go our way. After all, Ultimate Control is the ability to both pick up the pen and also let go of the pen. The long term effect of stress is, ultimately, illness. Your body is the foundation for everything you do in this life. It is the first thing we are taught to control as a child and the last thing over which we lose control when we pass to the next life. When one loses control of ones body and are in pain or discomfort, one realizes that nothing else matters in life, not friends, not family, not work nor money.

I am fortunate that I had to learn this lesson the hard way. It put me on the path of Enlightenment. I am grateful to all my great teachers. I can only hope that my children, loved ones, and friends will know what really counts, the Essences of Life, so they may be spared the same experience.

ς͡ɔGarry Choy

Wake up... Live the Life You Love,

On The Enlightened Path

Author Index

Burgess, Stephen A. *15*
Steve is a #1 best selling author, noted speaker, coach and consultant. He has a highly successful background, turning around and building extreme growth companies. He ensures the success of others who own, manage, or are starting small to medium businesses. He is CEO of Corporate Toolbelt, a consulting firm, Director of VIC Capital, a venture capital firm, founder of Speakers *Alive!,* a speakers agency, and serves on three Boards of Directors. His business advice is sought after by organizations and individuals alike.
Stephen A. Burgess
1-800-670-0520
steveburgess@ichoose2be.com
www.ichoose2be.com

Wake up... Live the Life You Love,

Burns, Sarah Chloe.. *7*

Sarah Chloe Burns is an historian, teaching at College of the Canyons in Santa Clarita, CA. She is an international lecturer who has presented to the Oxford Roundtable on Human Rights and Gender Discrimination (2003) and the Athens Institute of Education—ATINER—(2004). Her first book was published March 2004, and the article she presented to ATINER in December of 2004 will be published in the conference journal this year. Her biography is featured in the Marquis' *Who's Who: of American Women; in America; in American Education; and in the World.* She was named an International Woman of the Year by the International Biographical Association (Cambridge, England) in 2004.

Thanks immensely,
SARAH CHLOE BURNS,
Historian, Author, Lecturer
Web: http://www.history4sale.com
http://www.sarah4historyonline.com
Email: chloe@sarah4historyonline.com
scburns@bak.rr.com
Phone: 661-496-7114

Chopra, Dr. Deepak *41*

The Chopra Center for Well Being
7630 Fay Avenue
La Jolla, CA 92037
Fax: (858) 551-9570

On The Enlightened Path

Choy, Garry.. *113*

Garry is a dad, author, speaker, teacher, and mentor. He is happily married, has two wonderful boys, a degree in engineering and has traveled the world practicing and teaching the Tao, or natural way of life through Tai Chi for over 20 years. He has helped and healed many people along the way and is grateful to have made many new friends.
www.wisdomofgenerations.com
Burbank, California

Collins, Anita Bolen.. *19*

Please go to www.doorwaytoawakening.com for free how-to instructions on using muscle testing. If you'd like to receive a printed version, or wish to give this information to a friend, send one dollar to New Tool, c/o Anita Collins for your personal copy. Also at the website you'll find articles and resources to enhance your personal transformation and allow you to live with clarity in your life moment by moment. I wish you blessings along your path of awakening.
Anita Bolen Collins
PO Box 197, Parsippany, NJ 07054
www.doorwaytoawakening.com
Insight to Take You Beyond Mind into Being

Dyer, Wayne *27*

Best selling author and lecturer
Author of *Real Magic, Manifesting Your Destiny, Pulling Your Own Strings* and other books.
www.waynedyer.com

Wake up... Live the Life You Love,

Gaia, Laurelle Shanti **97**

Laurelle Shanti Gaia is a Director for The International Center for Reiki Training, and Founder of Infinite Light Healing Studies Center. Laurelle served as a founding member of the Council for Healing, and as a healer for a research project related to Spiritual Healing. She is the author of *The Book On Karuna*, *Be Peace Now*, and many published articles. Laurelle has also produced several meditation CDs. She can be contacted via email at IamInfiniteLight@aol.com or by mail at P.O. Box 1930, Sedona, AZ 86339

Gilman, Sara **23**

Together Sara Gilman and Diane Ulicsni have founded THE BRAIN COACHES! These dynamic Coaches have created unique, powerful, and effective tools to empower people around the world. Through their combined knowledge, training and experience, they have developed state of the art self hypnosis and guided imagery programs for you to use in your daily life. These programs are designed to ignite your Inner Coach and connect you to your Inner Spirit. Regular use of these programs will re-train your brain so you can break through the roadblocks of old information and create the life you love! Visit their website to learn more about speaking engagements, Coaching services, and life changing products. www.braincoaches.com
Sara@braincoaches.com
760-500-1173

On The Enlightened Path

Goncalves, Christina Reynolds.. *81*
My family moved to Brazil when I was 12 years old, thereby giving me exposure to an incredibly rich and beautiful culture. I became a physician in 1972, and went on to do 2 years of residency in OB/GYN, which I love. Ten years later, a friend introduced me to Classical Homeopathy and that has been my passion ever since. I've been married to the same wonderful husband for almost 40 years and we've gone through all sorts of challenges together. I have four amazing daughters and one grandson. Life seems to be redirecting me a little at this point in my career, so it looks like I'll be practicing Homeopathy part-time in Brazil (Curitiba), part-time in the US (San Diego), and anytime online! How about that? Big hug to you!
Christina Reynolds Goncalves, M.D.
Contact thru website: www.ChristinaRGoncalves.com

Gregg, Stephen.. *29*
InnerPrize
"Building Dreams, Changing Lives, Bringing Hope"
innerprize@hotmail.com
714-814-6888

Harper, Pamela, RN, CCH, CAC................................... *1*
Registered Nurse, Counselor, Hypnotherapist, Motivational Speaker, and maintains a private practice in San Clemente, CA.
Pamela@pamelaharper.com
www.universityofmasters.com
www.pamelaharper.com
toll free-866-5pamela

Wake up... Live the Life You Love,

Humphrey, John and Michelle.. *11*
Committed to making a difference! Professional Speakers
and Mindesigners, John and Michelle are Co-Founders of
the Effortless Living Institute and MIJODA Mindesign.
Their mission is to assist individuals, companies, and
professional athletes to achieve their inner most poten-
tial. Their top priority for their clients, RESULTS.
They believe without results everything is just theory.
They live in Southern California and travel the
world, speaking, training, and "walking their talk,"
inspiring others to get out there in life and create an absolute masterpiece. Destiny awaits.
John and Michelle Humphrey
Executive Mindesigners
The MIJODA Mindesign
Effortless Living Institute
3593 Granite Court
Carlsbad, CA 92010
(760) 720 – 1888
Michelle@LivingEffortless.com
John@LivingEffortless.com
www.LivingEffortless.com
www.mijodamindesign.com

Javdan, Sharon Shohreh.. *77*
Sharon is a cross-cultural and race relations consultant.
She is bi-cultural and multi-lingual. She has been the
owner of A New Human Race since 1990. A New Human
Race promotes "oneness of humanity" and "apprecia-
tion of diversity," through workshops, seminars, staff
training, and special materials. Sharon has an M.A. in
Teaching ESL and additional training in diversity.
Cross-cultural/Race Relations Consultant
and the Owner of A New Human Race
Specialized in "unity and diversity"
www.anewhumanrace.com
1-888-Nu-Human(Race) 1-888-684-8626

On The Enlightened Path

Larkin, Rahmana Lynn *33*

Rahmana Lynn Larkin MSW, ACSW, is a psychotherapist in private practice in Seattle, WA and a student of Sufism. She has written various articles on Sufi Psychology and other topics and has been a speaker at several venues including the Sufism Psychology Forum. In addition to her experience and training in Sufi Psychology, she is certified in Psychosynthesis, EMDR (Level 1&2), Reiki (Level 3), Hypnosis, and NLP. For more information please see www.transformationaltherapy.com. Lynn can be reached at (206) 915-4444 or Lynn@transformationaltherapy.com. For more information on Sufism please see www.ias.org.

Lynch, Jacqueline *109*

1117 N. Laurel Ave., #6
West Hollywood, CA 90046
tel (323) 654 6074
fax (323) 654 6075
Jacky@lynchIBM.com
www.lynchibm.com

Marconi, Lana *37*

Dr. Lana Marconi
Ph.D. in Energy Medicine
Th.D. in Transpersonal Psychology
www.drlana.com
1-800-Doc-Lana
Dr. Sandra Rose Michael
www.EnergyEnhancementSystem.com
(HI) 808-884-5644 (CA) 760-369-9636

Wake up... Live the Life You Love,

Morgan, Brandt *89*

Brandt is an author, teacher, coach, and Toltec mentor, trained by don Miguel Ruiz. Specializing in helping people find their true self and live their greatest dreams. He offers workshops, private coaching, and spirit journeys to places of power. Brandt is also the author of seven books, including the forthcoming *Vision Walk: Simple Steps to Inner Wisdom.*

Brandt Morgan
Your Guide to Living Your Dream
brandt@brandtmorgan.com
www.brandtmorgan.com

Morse, Dede, Ph.D. *43*

Vocalist
Clinical Psychologist
Author
www.dedemorse.com

Nguyen, Charles Hai *93*

P.O. Box 697
Lake Forest, CA 92609
949-716-9002
charles@financialsxpress.net
www.FinancialsXpress.com
To receive a FREE report on Charles' C's
to Success, please email your request to
charles@FromLoserToLeaderToLover.com or
visit www.FromLoserToLeaderToLover.com

On The Enlightened Path

O'Connor, Dave.. *47*

Dave O'Connor is 37 years old and has been working in the area of personal development for over 17 years. He is a certified master practitioner of NLP, and he has been trained in the new mind technology system called EDUCO™. EDUCO™ is the only success system in the world today that has been scientifically proven to work by a university and under its research conditions. He works with a special team of professional speakers and mind trainers from the UK and USA, dedicated to helping people design and manifest the life and world of their dreams. To find out more information, or to contact Dave, visit the websites below.

www.mijodamindesign.com
www.educomindpower.com
www.daveoconner.com
www.dave@livingeffortless.com
www.daveoc@lycos.com

Reid, Gregory Scott.. *85*

The Millionaire Mentor
 # 1 best selling author, speaker, and radio personality,
www.AlwaysGood.com
GregReid@AlwaysGood.com
www.misterkeynote.com

Reynolds, Carolyn P., MS.................................... *51*

Feng Shui Consultant, San Diego, CA
Tel. (858) 496-3345
www.CarolynPReynolds.com

Wake up... Live the Life You Love,

Ruiz, don Miguel..5

We are honored to include, co-author don Miguel Ruiz and a segment from his best selling book, *The Four Agreements*.

Don Miguel Ruiz is a Master of the Toltec mystery school tradition. For more than a decade he has worked to impart wisdom of the ancient Toltec to his students and apprentices, guiding them toward their personal freedom. He continues to offer a unique blend of ancient wisdom and modern-day awareness through lectures, workshops, and journeys to sacred sites around the world. For further information, please contact:

Sixth Sun Journeys of the Spirit
P.O. Box 1846
Carlsbad, CA 92018-1846
800-924-3203
www.miguelruiz.com

Salehi, Nasrin.. *105*

Nasrin, born in Tehran, Iran, is a mother, wife, teacher, and a full-time student in the University of Life. She is an explorer in the field of interfaith spiritual growth. She is also a Holistic life style coach and serves as a counselor at the Center for Family and Children Services, as well as in the Crisis Center for Women. Nasrin is certified in hypnosis and feng-shui.

Contact information:
Tel: 760-438-7338 or 760-412-2472
Fax: 760-476-0214
E-mail: www.nazkoda2000@yahoo.com

Steven E.

stevene@wakeuplive.com
Creator of the number one, best-selling series, *Wake Up...Live the Life You Love.*

On The Enlightened Path

Sirovy, Mina Jo, Dr. *55*

Dr. Mina Sirovy has been practicing psychotherapy for 22 years in Oceanside, Vista, Carlsbad, and Encinitas, CA. She specializes in hypnosis, guided meditations, Eye Movement Desensitization for traumas, relationship counseling, and Electromagnetic Field Balancing. She's been published in three meditation books and has been named to Who's Who since 1995. In her counseling, Soul Needs are of paramount importance.
Contact information:
drmina@cox.net
Phone or fax: 760-967-6100
3678 Seaflower Lane
Oceanside, CA 92056

Smith, Colin *59*

It took a life changing, emotional experience to motivate me to contact a naturopath to assist me to overcome my poor health issues and to lose 47 kilos. I noticed that I was taking my own personal responsibility for my own overall health. When I reflect on the lives of others: What I want for myself, I want for others.
Website: www.colinsmithpublishing.com.au
Personal contact: cols8@bigpond.com
Postal: Lot 157, Wills Road, PO Box 314
Emerald, 4720, Queensland, Australia
Ph: +61-74982-0912
Fax: +61-74982-0913

Nicholson-Spears, Yolande *101*

Yolande Nicholson-Spears is the Vice President of Education and Community Relations at The Bushnell Center for the Performing Arts in Hartford, Connecticut. She is also a writer, playwright, public speaker, and career transition coach. Her e-mail addresses are ynspears@juno.com and YolandeSpears@bushnell.org

For your free gift, go to: **www.wakeupand.com**

Wake up... Live the Life You Love,

Striker, Debbie.. *63*

Debbie currently crafts stained glass art that expresses
Spirituality and Beauty in their boundless facets. Her cre-
ations can be found in private collections all over the world.
One of her favorite projects to date was a set of 4 wind
chimes created for an indoor garden in a Hong Kong shopping center. She was one of two stained glass artists chosen
to create them. Her husband John, contributes his artistic
talents by designing for her glasswork, as well as carving
walking staffs and wands. Their website features many other
"Spirit Crafted" artists, and a percentage of every sale is
donated to the Leukemia & Lymphoma Society.

Stained Glass Artisan / CEO
TGlass Studios
PO Box 391
Haymarket, VA 20168
Create@tglass.net
www.tglass.net

Valdes, Jodi M. *65*

Jodi is a Reconnective Healing™ Practitioner and Certified
Soul Coach. She is the co-founder of World Village, an
outdoor marketplace, assisting low-income families through
micro-enterprise. Jodi is also the founder of The Center for
Indigo Living. She is the author of the forthcoming book,
Indigo Dog, helping bridge parents and Indigo children.
Jodi is a graduate of the University of Texas at Austin.

indigoanimals@aol.com
Centerforindigoliving.com
The Center for Indigo Living
1643 6th Ave. #314
San Diego, CA 92101
619-667-0212

On The Enlightened Path

Wasinger, Christian, CCH *69*
Certified Clinical Hypnotherapist,
NLP-Master Practitioner
Results Coach, Author, Speaker, and Lecturer
San Diego, CA
www.ChristianWasinger.com
Please look for my upcoming book which will not only be
an enlightened ABC's, but also an enlightened dictionary.

Winkle, Bruce.. *73*
Energy Healer and Teacher (People and Horses)
Creator of Energetic Wellness for Horses
Celebrant of Horse Awakenings
703-771-7755
www.BRUCEWINKLE.COM

Wake up... Live the Life You Love,